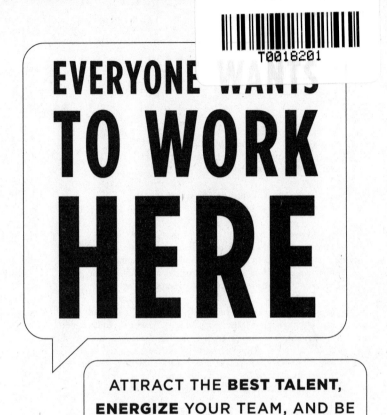

EVERYONE WANTS TO WORK HERE

ATTRACT THE **BEST TALENT**, **ENERGIZE** YOUR TEAM, AND BE THE **LEADER** IN YOUR MARKET

MAURA NEVEL THOMAS

simple **truths**

▶ Small books. BIG IMPACT.

Published by Simple Truths, an imprint of Sourcebooks
P.O. Box 4410, Naperville, Illinois 60567-4410
(630) 961-3900
sourcebooks.com

Library of Congress Cataloging-in-Publication
Data is on file with the publisher.

Printed and bound in the United States of America.
SB 10 9 8 7 6 5 4 3 2

In loving memory of Florence and John Dovidio, whose love, support, and generosity made all the difference. And to my godmother, Marie, whose endless source of support and cheerleading always help to keep my self-doubt in check.

Contents

Introduction: The Shift to Knowledge Work vii

1   **The Most Important Job
of a Leader Is to Think** 1

2   **How Leaders Can Spend More Time "On"
the Business than "In" the Business** 14

3   **Changing a Culture of Urgency** 40

4   **Fast Doesn't Equal Better** 45

5   **A Leadership Formula to Empower Teams** 57

6   **Take Vacation Seriously** 71

7 How Remote and Hybrid
Work Are Changing Business   98

8 Necessary Commitments for Successful
Remote and Hybrid Teams   111

9 The Problem with Synchronous
Communication and Remote Work   121

10 Work-Life Balance   137

11 The New Realities of Office Work   156

12 Measuring the Productivity
of Knowledge Work   168

Conclusion: Create Your Culture with Intention   178
Let's Continue the Conversation   181
Acknowledgments   182
Notes   183
Index   187
About the Author   190

Introduction

The Shift to Knowledge Work

In the Industrial Age, work happened within the walls of a factory. Today, knowledge work is the product of our brains, and that work has increasingly left the confines of an office. Corporate offices have moved to cubicle environments, open floor plans, "hot desks," and—the biggest and most disruptive shift since the start of the coronavirus pandemic—a variety of remote work options.

In addition, traditional work relationships continue to change. The freelance work platform Upwork reports that in 2021, 51 percent of college graduates were engaged in skilled freelance work, up 6 percent from 2020, and 56 percent of non-freelancers reported that they expect to freelance in the future.[i]

The most vexing challenge in the wake of the pandemic seems to be the struggle to keep work from becoming all-consuming, with remote work being described less as "working from home" and more as "living where you work."

Leaders often fail to recognize that high-quality knowledge work is incompatible with the pace and expectations of most work environments. When the optimal work environment is provided, individuals become more successful and more engaged, which allows leaders and organizations to gain a competitive advantage and improvements to the bottom line.

So what is knowledge work?

Knowledge work, for the purposes of this book, is defined as work for which "thinking" is the raw material. The products of knowledge work are intangible brain outputs like communications, information, complex decisions, analysis, planning, and critical thinking.

If thinking is a raw material of knowledge work, then the environment in which that thinking is executed is relevant. The thinking environment is formed by how individual knowledge workers feel about their tasks and their jobs overall and by how well the tool they use to produce the thinking—their brain—is performing. These two things mean that workers' personal well-being should be attended to. In fact, multiple studies show that caring leaders create better results.[ii]

KNOWLEDGE WORK DEFINITION

· ·

There is an argument to be made that there are different types of knowledge work, and I would agree. For example, there is knowledge work for which the primary outputs are specifically the product of thinking. Writers, designers, and other creative types, senior executives in charge of ideas and strategy, and software developers are some examples of this type of knowledge worker. A broader definition of knowledge work includes more task-oriented positions, such as administrative staff. These roles still have more in common with knowledge work than manufacturing or other industrial work, so when I refer to knowledge workers, I'm including office workers in general.

> **Most leaders are unaware of how much impact their everyday behaviors have on the organizational culture and how seemingly innocent decisions can negatively impact the lives of their employees.**

Considerations of Knowledge Work

In this book, I'll discuss many factors that determine the productivity and success of knowledge work, including the following:

→   the influence of leadership

→   the unique needs of knowledge work with regard to optimal functioning of our brains, including both physical and emotional well-being

→   the increasing importance of attention, simultaneous with the rise of endless distractions

→   the proliferation of communication and the nature of urgency that surrounds it

→ the growing importance of disconnected time

→ the complications of a fully distributed (remote) workforce, or a "hybrid" workforce, where some or all team members work from somewhere other than a company office some or all of the time

→ corporate culture as it relates to the support or the detriment of all these issues

I rarely meet leaders who intentionally create a toxic culture, but most leaders are unaware of how much impact their everyday behaviors have on the organizational culture and how seemingly innocent decisions can negatively impact the lives of their employees. The culture of an organization is created by the collective behaviors of every employee who works at the organization, but the influence each individual has on the culture is not equal. Leadership behaviors tend to shape the culture more than any others, because employees naturally (although often unconsciously) model the behaviors of their boss and other leaders in the organization.

Unconscious Calculations

In my work, I'm often struck by what I call "unconscious calculations." These are habits and behaviors we engage in based on conclusions that aren't made consciously or intentionally.

Here are four examples, with more to follow throughout the book:

→ **Constant work:** Few people would admit to wanting to work 24/7/365. Yet most people never disconnect and are continually available to work communication (email, chat, text, etc.).

→ **Success metrics:** Rarely is "number of hours spent working" a stated metric for performance evaluation. Yet a study done by Stanford showed that while remote workers are 13 percent more productive, their promotion rates are much lower than those who spent most of their work hours in the office.[iii]

→ **Multitasking:** Decades of research show that multitasking is not more effective or more efficient. Yet this is the typical state of work for most professionals, and it still frequently appears in job descriptions.

→ **Vacation:** Studies show that employees tend to believe that vacation offers important benefits,[iv] but two out of three employees work while on vacation.[v]

One result of the current work environment—and these unconscious calculations—is that too many workers are exhausted. Exhausted workers mean exhausted companies, exhausted families, exhausted communities, and an exhausted world. The bottom line for busy professionals struggling to regain control over their lives and for the companies that employ them is that *exhaustion is optional*, and it's not conducive to quality outcomes for knowledge work.

I believe the way we look at work needs an overhaul, and this overhaul will only happen if it's modeled by leaders. My work is guided by a specific definition of productivity from the dictionary: achieving a significant result. So the productivity—of an individual knowledge worker or an organization—in a given time frame is the extent to which progress is made on things that are considered significant.

Individual knowledge worker productivity can't be assessed only at the micro level; a macro view is also relevant. For example, if a worker meets deadlines, produces superior results for the organization, and achieves objectives but works too much and hates her job, is her "productivity" sustainable? And will the short-term gains the organization realized be wiped out if (when) she becomes disengaged, burns out, quits, or requires an extended leave?

The Gift of Leadership

Everyone knows that leaders influence their employees' work lives, but virtually every leader I speak with has missed the extent to which they influence their employees' personal lives, families, communities, and ultimately the world. If that seems like an overstatement, I think this section will surprise you.

The point of this book is to offer leaders a blueprint for creating a productive culture, where all knowledge workers can contribute their best selves and their best work every day, and an important component of this productive work culture is the way leaders interact with team members. This interaction includes many components that we will discuss in this section:

→ clarity of roles and responsibilities
→ assignment of tasks and projects
→ organization of information
→ autonomy
→ trust
→ control over workload
→ identifying skills gaps and offering professional development opportunities
→ modeling productive behaviors
→ clarifying and enforcing policies, procedures, and intended norms
→ efficient communication
→ dependable "face time"

→ recognition and accountability

→ mentoring

→ psychological safety

Many are familiar with the saying that "employees don't quit companies, they quit bosses." Like much conventional wisdom, this saying certainly contains some truth. It's easy to understand how leaders (anyone who supervises any employees directly) would influence whether an employee is happy or unhappy at work.

The research shows that employees actually quit their jobs for a variety of reasons. A more accurate way to understand why employees are unhappy at work is provided by McKinsey, whose research shows that an employee's relationship with management is a top factor in their job satisfaction and the *second most important factor in employees' overall well-being.*[vi] [Emphasis mine.]

This underscores the point of this section: **leaders underestimate the influence they have on employees' whole lives, not just their lives at work**. When people are stressed out and unhappy at work, those feelings tend to infect their personal lives. The converse is also true: when people are happy and satisfied at work, they tend to be happier overall. Either set of feelings will naturally impact the employee's immediate family, so leaders impact not only an employee's work life but also their home life.

Impact on Families

Impacting an employee's home life means leaders have influence over an employee's family. Studies show, for example, that just the expectation that an employee *might* receive an email from their boss after hours causes stress not only for the employee, but also for the employee's family. Imagine the situation where family members have an expectation of a family event: a family meal, a trip, or other opportunities to spend time together. But those plans disintegrate as soon as the email or phone call is received that brings news of an "issue" at work. Now the family is having dinner without Dad's attention, because he is tapping out emails on his phone, or now the family is going to Disneyland without Mom, who had to work instead. Or maybe Mom still tags along on the trip, but is waving from the sidelines while on the phone dealing with the work "emergency." When I relate these scenarios in my leadership sessions, it's not uncommon for one or more participants in the room to get emotional because these experiences are all too familiar. Can you think of an example of this in your own family?

> **Leaders need to recognize their influence as a gift, and wield that influence wisely.**

Impact on the World

Another example of a leader's influence outside work is when employees are so exhausted at the end of their workday that they have very little left over to give their families or communities. They work late or need to spend time "unwinding" after a stressful day at the office so they miss the opportunity to participate in bath time, homework, or movie night. Or they work such long hours, or come home from work so exhausted, that they will never say yes to community involvement like serving on a nonprofit board, coaching a Little League team, directing the school play, or being a scout or other troop leader. This is the impact leaders have on communities. And if a leader impacts an employee, their family, and their community, then they impact the world. When I share this point in my leadership training sessions, the recognition of this impact is powerful. It's truly an aha moment.

My work is about helping leaders recognize their influence as a gift, and wield that influence wisely.

1

The Most Important Job of a Leader Is to Think

In the introduction, I discussed how the most important outcome of a leader's interaction with their team is influence—over employees' lives, communities, and ultimately the world. Of course they also have influence over the operations of their department or organization. But the most important job of a leader is thinking. This book is written primarily for leaders of knowledge workers, those who work most often in an office at a computer, and whose outputs include planning, brainstorming, analyzing, and problem-solving. Another job of leaders is to consider a broad view of company processes so they can implement an organized, thoughtful, and coordinated approach to work as it moves through the organization.

An Elevated Approach to Leadership

Leaders must spend more time than most currently do, on elevating their view of the organization and offering a more thoughtful approach to management. This is certainly true in senior leadership positions, but it's also true at a more supervisory level. The leaders closest to the day-to-day operations are in the best position to improve operations when they have the opportunity to take a step outside the day-to-day "doing" and do more thinking. As opposed to the random, communication-based approach to work that is common in many organizations, there are multiple benefits to the organized, coordinated, thoughtful approaches to work that will be discussed in this book. This thoughtful approach to the operations they are responsible for offers a variety of unexpected indirect benefits. Here are some of the direct benefits you can achieve by applying the advice in this book.

Drastically reduce the volume of communication in the organization. Instead of hiding in individual email inboxes, all relevant information will be centralized, organized, and easily accessible to everyone. This benefits not only the current project but also future, similar projects.

Slow down the pace of the organization and reduce the stress on all team members. For knowledge work especially, a less-stressful work environment offers more time for what psychologist Daniel Kahneman calls "slow" or "system

2 thinking." In his bestselling book *Thinking, Fast and Slow*, Kahneman explains that system 1 thinking is automatic; you have little or no control over it—often the way we dash off immediate responses to chat and email messages. System 1 thinking is fast and effortless, but also occurs without self-awareness and is more likely to be irrational, impulsive, and affected by bias. System 2 thinking is slow and effortful, but it's also more deliberate, conscious, and rational, and it seeks new and missing information. He says we typically think we have reasons for what we do (i.e., our actions are the result of system 2 thinking), but in reality, we spend the majority of our time in system 1 thinking, which is often more likely to lead to mistakes.

Keep the big picture accessible and regarded in context as the project progresses. This helps reinforce the reasons that the work is considered important, and offers clarity about the value each team member brings to the team and the organization. Meaningful work is important to motivation and employee engagement, and it impacts an organization's bottom line. For example, research has found that 80 percent of attendees at the Conference for Women said they would rather have a boss who cared about them finding meaning and success in work than receive a 20 percent pay increase, and employees with very meaningful work spend one additional hour per week working and take two fewer days of paid leave per year.[i] (While this is not necessarily beneficial to their well-being, I believe the point of the research was to illustrate that meaningful work corresponds to dedication to one's job.)

Minimize the necessity for extended workdays in order to improve work-life balance and reduce burnout. When employees spend their days working from their inboxes or their chat apps (like Slack and Teams), they need after-hours time to get their "real work" done. Or even worse, many employees report to me that they spend the majority of their daytime in meetings and a majority of their after-hours time getting on top of their communication, so "real work" is frequently squeezed out. This puts them in a perpetual state of stress from feeling behind and watching their to-do lists get ever longer, while rarely feeling the satisfaction that comes from the accomplishment of important—but thoughtful and time-consuming—tasks. With a more structured, organized, and coordinated approach to work dissemination, where information is accessible to all in a self-serve way, team members can spend the majority of their workdays actually *doing* their most important work, the need for meetings is minimized, and the volume of communication is drastically reduced so after-hours work time is rarely necessary.

All team members can spend their days being thoughtfully proactive rather than haphazardly reactive. "Spending less time being reactive and more time being proactive" is one of the most frequent reasons cited by my clients for bringing me in to deliver productivity training to their teams, and one of the most frequent benefits of my work that team members cite when asked how my training helped them. When knowledge workers can be less reactive, they feel more in control of their work. Higher perceived control is associated with lower levels of depression, fewer functional limitations, and better health, wealth, wisdom, life satisfaction, optimism, and cognitive performance (e.g., better memory or ability to pursue goals).[ii]

Increasing both the quality and the quantity of work makes team members feel satisfied and productive at the end of their workdays. Progress is an important factor in motivation and fulfillment,[iii] and the reported "Great Resignation" brought on by the pandemic is said to be caused in part by knowledge workers rethinking the role of work and the satisfaction they get from it compared to other aspects of their lives.[iv] Research aligns with my experience working with clients: greater productivity and satisfaction in work ultimately make employees happier and more engaged, and reduce organizational turnover.

Employees have more space to be physically and emotionally fit, and have more to offer their families and communities because they have less pressure and stress at work. Lower stress has benefits that carry over to all parts of an employee's life and frees them up not only to take better care of themselves physically, but also to do other things that nourish their spirit, like spending time with family and volunteering in their community. This will feed their creativity and their motivation when they are back at the job. I'll show you exactly how to achieve all these results in the following chapters.

Brainpower Momentum

All the job outputs identified so far are the result of thinking, where brainpower is the raw material. This thinking work is what Georgetown professor Cal Newport defines as "deep work" (in his book of the same name), requiring "the ability to focus without distraction on a cognitively demanding task." He says that the benefit is that "it allows you to quickly master complicated information and produce better results in less time." *Mastering complicated information* is the thinking work, and the *better results in less time* are the planning, analysis, and other knowledge work outputs listed above.

I think about deep work as needing "brainpower

momentum." It takes time to get started, get focused, and fully mobilize our resources in the service of our most important, most meaningful work. By "resources," I mean not only our knowledge, wisdom, and experience, but also our empathy, passion, kindness, diligence, and all the other qualities we bring to our day-to-day lives to make them unique, richer, and more impactful.

Consider this analogy: imagine your task is to ride a bicycle for ten miles, as quickly and efficiently as you can. You begin to pedal, and just as you build up speed and start making progress, something unexpectedly makes you hit the brakes. Because you had to stop, you've lost your momentum and have to expend more effort to get going again. Imagine you are forced to brake every time you start to go faster. You can never coast. You have to pedal—hard—all the time. How much longer do you think it will take to get to your destination? How much more energy will you have to expend to get there? How much more difficult and frustrating do you think the ride will be? Imagine a bicycle race, and how the professional cyclists come cruising over the finish line, looking sleek and effortless. Then imagine those who bring up the rear, hours after the professionals come over the finish line—breathing heavy, swerving all over the road, working hard to move those pedals to reach the finish line.

Those laggard cyclists represent your brainpower on distraction. The constant interruptions we allow throughout our workdays prevent brainpower momentum, requiring us to expend extra effort and work longer. The result is sloppy performance as we are unable to build the brainpower momentum we need to unleash our genius. In the end, we're left with unsatisfying, unfulfilling workdays full of diversions not only from our daily goals, but also ultimately from the path that we determine for our lives.

Distraction Undermines Thinking

The problem's not just that we're getting distracted from work; it's also that we're getting distracted from important work *by other work*. We often sit down to do thoughtful, in-depth tasks only to be lured away by incoming emails from clients or colleagues. Faced with the flood of incoming information, interruptions, and distractions, many knowledge workers are so overwhelmed that we spend much of our time "playing defense," we're less able to identify priorities, and we stay mostly in reactive mode. Work comes at us from half a dozen places all at once, so it's easy for us to get quickly overwhelmed trying to remember and manage it.

The pace is frantic with a new interruption every few minutes, so it feels like there is no time to stop and organize it all. In fact, we are distracted so often that in the increasingly rare absence of constant distraction, we find ourselves bored, and we seek out distraction! The environment chips away at our attention span until we rarely or never have the patience to do only one thing at a time, so we constantly check email, instant messages, social media pages, etc., to pounce on anything that seems to need a response, providing convenient justification for our need for distraction.

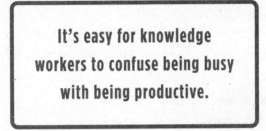

It's easy for knowledge workers to confuse being busy with being productive.

Additionally, these communication channels often bring new tasks and details at a fast and frantic pace, so workers often operate without a clear picture of their total responsibilities. Instead, they flit between email, voicemail, meeting notes, and their various haphazard to-do lists to try to keep track of priorities. Since most workers have no clear plan, it's faster and easier to spend the majority of their time reacting to what happens to them rather than proactively tracking and acting on the most important or the highest-impact activities. It's easy for knowledge workers to confuse being busy with being productive when faced with this combination of a frantic pace, a lack of clarity over responsibilities and priorities, and constant distractions reinforcing the urge to multitask.

Indeed, when employees are constantly task switching (what we think of as multitasking), thoughtful work is impeded, so productivity suffers. Studies show that multitasking causes tasks to take longer, and it causes the quality of the work to be lower. Constant multitasking makes us more prone to making mistakes, more likely to miss important information and cues, and less likely to retain information in working memory, which impairs problem-solving and creativity.[v]

Constant reactivity also deprives employees of the quiet, uninterrupted time they need to do their most meaningful work and even of the pauses they need to recharge their brains. People need what neuroscientists call *controlled attention* to do thoughtful work such as writing, planning, creating, and strategizing. They also need the pauses, when there isn't too much stimulus and they aren't trying to focus on anything in particular. This is *restorative attention*, and it's the quiet time the brain needs to process information. It's often when insights are generated.

For knowledge workers, downtime is key, both away from the office and at work, in the form of breaks and the space to be reflective and thoughtfully proactive. Since the product of knowledge work is the creation, distribution, or application of knowledge, knowledge work outputs improve with a fresh perspective, which can't be achieved if we never fully disconnect from work.[vi] Knowledge workers also benefit from continual learning, which is impeded by constant distraction. Learning occurs only when information is absorbed in a focused and meaningful way. You hired your knowledge workers for the edge their wisdom, experience, and ability to learn would give your business, not for how many tasks they can seemingly do at once or how many emails they can answer in a day.

Yet this is how most knowledge workers (including leaders) spend their time. In most professional jobs today, multitasking has become a coping strategy. We are constantly shifting our attention among a variety of activities, like trying to complete assignments and projects, tracking and responding to endless digital communications, and managing interruptions from colleagues and the office bustle.

Constant distraction leaves a trail of scattered thoughts and partly done tasks in its wake. It leaves us feeling overwhelmed and tired. And when our busy, exhausting days don't come with a sense of accomplishment, our work feels unsatisfying at best—and demotivating at worst. This is a recipe for burnout because progress is what drives us, and accomplishment makes us feel happy and satisfied.

In my work as a productivity trainer and speaker for thousands of organizations, I have found that distraction is the single biggest barrier to meaningful, satisfying, thoughtful work. Studies by Gloria Mark and colleagues show that we often switch what we're doing every few minutes, and these frequent interruptions "cause us to work faster, which causes more stress, higher frustration, time pressure, and effort."[vii] And this sabotages not just our performance but also the way we show up in the world.

Designed for Distraction

In most audiences, the majority of people tell me they have more than one computer monitor on their desk. Sometimes, the extra computer screen "real estate" is useful in the service of one task, like a designer who has design tools on one monitor and the piece being designed on the other monitor. But my audience members also admit that the way they use their two (or more!) monitors most of the time is so they can have their actual work (a proposal, spreadsheet, document, etc.) on one monitor, and their communication channels (typically email and chat at least) on the other monitor. The arrival of a new message is indicated typically by sound or motion, both of which pull their attention away.

Most knowledge workers receive a message every few minutes, so it's fair to say that we switch our attention every few minutes—by design! And when confronted with this reality, my audience members both recognize the futility and feel powerless to change it. They believe that their work requires them to review every message as it arrives in an effort to be "responsive," keep customers happy, and deal with "emergencies." While it's true that employees are not *actually* powerless and *can* take steps to address this independently, the culture of the organization and the behavior of the leaders often contribute to those feelings of powerlessness. In upcoming sections, I'll provide ideas for how leaders can help employees with this challenge.

2

How Leaders Can Spend More Time "On" the Business than "In" the Business

In my experience with my corporate clients, the day-to-day interactions of the team and the leader indicate that the leader's job is to put out the "fires" that come up: when an absence or a departure disrupts a deliverable timeline, when a client or customer is upset, when a supplier fails to keep a commitment, or when some other piece of the production or the operation fails to execute according to plan. These issues are usually run up the chain of command, and each level of employee makes a determination about getting their boss involved. Especially in small and midsize companies and at the department level in larger organizations, I rarely see the leader who declines to get involved if asked, or who doesn't want to get involved when they become aware of the problem.

My leadership clients tell me that one of the biggest impediments to getting their work done is unexpected "emergencies." Without an intentional effort to analyze these emergencies and create processes and contingency plans, organizations are doomed to repeat the same mistakes, and unexpected emergencies become the norm rather than the exception.

Embrace the Big Picture

What if there were a more effective approach for a leader than getting involved? What if you stepped back and took a higher level look at the situation? If you considered how to prevent the problems before they arose, or how to avoid the same issue occurring again in the future? This is often described as working "on" the business instead of "in" the business. And to be sure, the distinction between a manager and a leader is important here: it may indeed be the role of some managers to "fight these fires." But the more leadership responsibility one has (or the more useful a manager wants to be), the more time they should spend "on" the business instead of "in" it. When leaders spend more time analyzing and organizing operations, this broader perspective of the organization offers the following benefits:

→ A focus on continuous improvement of business operations.

→ Increased efficiency in processes and procedures over time.

→ A reservoir of "learned knowledge" from which the organization can benefit in the future.

→ Team members who learn, grow, and become less dependent on their boss, by making their own decisions and earning experience.

→ Leaders who offer exponentially more value to the organization.

The next sections will discuss ways to elevate your leadership from being *in* the day-to-day operations to working *on* more efficient operations.

Examine How Work Gets Done

The first way to elevate your leadership is to prevent future "fires." Look at the way work flows through your department or organization (depending on the scope of your responsibilities). How do your team members determine what they should work on during the day? How do they prioritize? Is their work process intentional and methodical, flowing out from team initiatives? Or do employees receive work primarily via constant and haphazard requests from colleagues, vendors, and clients via their numerous communication channels, like email and chat?

> **Trying to stay on top of constant communication squeezes out time to move important projects forward.**

The latter puts employees in a difficult situation, especially if there is an emphasis in the organization on being "responsive" to internal and external communication. Team members likely feel pressure to stay on top of these messages, offering support and completing tasks that are asked of them. But these requests typically come in all day long, so "staying on top of them" squeezes out time to move *their* important projects forward. Even when the communications are related to their important projects, constantly switching from project to project in a disorganized manner is extremely inefficient and encourages a micro-level perspective rather than a macro-level perspective.

This inefficient approach to working is unfortunately also appealing, because everyone likes to feel needed and helpful, and answering emails and chats is often faster and easier than tackling those big projects in a thoughtful way. This is how driven professionals end up spending their days being very busy but not very productive—when by *productive*, I mean making progress on significant results.

This approach to work emphasizes the details and ignores the big picture, and is unproductive in several ways, including the following:

→   It eliminates the opportunity to see relationships between projects.

→   It obscures problems that may be lurking a few steps away in the process, which propagates these unexpected emergencies.

→   It delays timelines.

→   It contributes to extended work hours, with employees often feeling "the only time to get my work done is at night when no one is bothering me!"

→   It makes people feel frazzled and stressed by causing a

constant shift from one problem, issue, and person to another all day long.

→ It causes team members to end their workdays feeling unsatisfied, and like they didn't really accomplish anything.

It's the leader's job to assess how their team members receive work, and to make sure that ad hoc requests from inside or outside the team don't derail workers' ability to make important progress on their priorities. A goal to aim for, though difficult to achieve, is that employees *could* work for days at a time without communicating in real time with anyone else.

Make Information Self-Serve (Asynchronous)

The second way to elevate your leadership relates to how your team members receive information. To be clear, I'm not recommending that team members *avoid* communicating with each other, only that the leader creates a shift away from constant, real-time communication (synchronous) to a process where information is self-serve and therefore asynchronous: project details, timelines, and statuses are organized and centralized in a place that all team members can access. This typically includes one or more locations such as project management tools and shared drives.

So as an employee goes through their list of tasks and projects assigned by their boss or dictated by their job responsibilities, all relevant information necessary to do that work is accessible to them, and needing to interrupt someone else to move their work forward is the exception rather than the rule. And even when a piece of information *is* needed, the request can be made asynchronously—a delay in receiving an answer to their request does not hold up their work.

Advice in Action

Individual contributors can help move their team toward working in a way that is more organized and coordinated, but ultimately it's the leader's job to manage how work gets done in their department or their organization.

This is an undertaking for which there is no one right way, but in the following section, I will provide some examples of how you can successfully shift from mostly synchronous communication to mostly asynchronous communication and some factors to consider if you decide to invest in making this shift at your organization. It's also important to recognize that with any improvement effort, there is always room for *more* improvement. You may never reach a "perfect" state of efficiency or excellence, but in my experience with clients, even incremental improvements produce magnified benefits.

First I'll share the changes we made on my team of two full-time employees plus six regular, retainer-based but part-time contractors. Then I'll profile a more traditional organization that follows the same principles but on a larger scale.

Example: Regain Your Time Team Operations

My company, Regain Your Time, is a family business, where my partner (in business and in life), Shawn, and I are full-time, salaried employees, and my mother is one of six regular, part-time contractors. We also have a reserve of trusted, project-based contractors whom we call on as needed. We have greatly increased the efficiency and decreased the volume of the team communication over time, but like most things, it's a work in progress, and we are still working on a more efficient way to track project status.

CONTRACTORS VS. EMPLOYEES

· ·

There's a challenge for teams made up of part-time independent contractors that is lessened when the team members are all full-time employees, namely that each independent contractor has their own tools and processes for tracking their work. The extent to which they can conform to the tools and processes used by one client is limited by their need to accommodate many clients.

As our team came together over the years, the primary communication channel was email. But as the company grew, new (contract) team members were brought on, roles got larger in scope, and the time they spent working with us increased. With this growth also came an increase in the volume of our communication. Soon I needed to communicate with team members not only individually, but also in groups. Additionally, they began to need to communicate with each other, where I only had an indirect role—being aware of what they were working on but not needing to be directly involved. It quickly became apparent to me that we were being weighed down by long email threads containing multiple people that seemed to demand "reply all" to keep everyone in the loop. My inbox was a mix of "just keeping you in the loop—no action required" messages and "we're waiting for you to get back to us on this" messages. It was hard for me to recognize, sort, and act on them appropriately. As the team grew, I spent more and more time processing my email.

Further complicating our communication was the fact that our team members are all independent business owners working on their own flexible schedules. Everyone works different times and divides their time among several clients, so I can't expect anyone to be available at a moment's notice. Out-of-control, inefficient communication is a problem I see frequently, and increasingly so with the rise of remote and hybrid work and the resulting elimination of "business hours." This challenge is also faced by global teams who work across different—sometimes even opposite—time zones.

It can be less apparent in the day-to-day, because the volume of dozens, sometimes more than a hundred, emails on a daily basis often seems "normal." But after returning from a weeklong vacation to over five hundred messages in my inbox, I decided to do an analysis of the types of messages I was receiving, with the goal of minimizing the volume just for the next time I went on vacation. But I quickly realized I could consistently reduce the volume of messages I received and increase the efficiency of our communication, whether I was on vacation or not.

As a result of my analysis, we made one primary change and one more subtle change that have improved the productivity and efficiency of the team. The primary change was that I implemented a team communication tool designed specifically for asynchronous communication and adopted the behaviors that would make it optimally useful.

The more subtle changes that are still in process include holding the team more accountable to meeting deadlines. When we're all in agreement as to when requests of each other are due, and we know that we will be held accountable to those commitments, less communication is necessary.

The Process Matters More Than the Tools

When teaching individuals my Empowered Productivity™ system for personal workflow management, I help them realize that my definition of a "system" is primarily the collection of habits and behaviors, not an app or software. A lot of attendees come to my trainings frustrated by the fact that they've tried lots of apps and software, but none have really helped them. That's like expecting that if you tried to play golf with the same clubs a PGA pro uses, they would make you play golf just like that pro. It's how you *use* the tools that makes the difference, both in sports and for improving personal productivity.

The same lesson can be applied to organizational processes. I see many organizations that implement digital tools to improve the efficiency of their operations, but the leaders get frustrated because the apps and software either don't get used or don't produce the intended results.

For leaders to make the work of their department more organized and coordinated—and less chaotic and reactive—relying on tools like apps and software is not sufficient. The new communication processes you put in place must include effective behaviors for storing, organizing, and retrieving team-wide or organization-wide information, because this is typically the information the team requires to do their work. The following chapters will offer many suggestions for how to make information more transparent and accessible to others.

Habits for Team Communication

Two common ways for teams to share information are via chat and email. But in my experience, the habits for using email and chat tools are left to the individuals to decide. Often there are no guidelines for how the team communicates. Individual communication behaviors come about by necessity and expediency rather than through deliberation and planning. In many organizations, the internally accessible repository for information that team members need to do their jobs does not exist. So whenever someone needs a piece of information, they must ask someone else—by email, chat, or often both! That information, which is likely needed by other team members as well, is then "hidden" in individual files or inboxes that are not accessible to others.

> **It's not apps and software tools that create efficiencies or inefficiencies. It's how the team uses the tools.**

When information is sent via chat, a benefit is that it can be more accessible to others. But often requests are made in the most expedient way rather than the most organized way. Another problem with both email and chat is that they are treated—often by the sender *and* the receiver—as synchronous channels. This means the sender expects an immediate response, and the receiver is interrupted via some audible or visual notification that the message was received and, once distracted from their other work, adopts the expectation that the response needs to be immediate.

I'd like to emphasize again that everything I've described in this section—the methods for sharing information, the disruption caused by the communication, and the expectations of the senders and the receivers—are all behaviors and habits. The apps and software are not the cause of the inefficiencies. The behaviors are. Said another way, it's not the tools but how the team *uses* the tools.

With no guidance from leaders about how to communicate efficiently, individuals choose very different behaviors, and the inefficiencies spiral out of control. These poor communication behaviors create three types of inefficiency: the excessive volume of communication inside the organization, the level of distraction caused by the communication, and the disorganization of the information shared in the messages.

→ **Volume:** The more communication team members receive, the more time they need to spend being reactive and the less time they have to do thoughtful, proactive work.

→ **Distraction:** In my experience, professionals think they need to respond to communication very fast or even immediately, and feel pressure to do so. Unless the leadership emphasizes that communication is low priority or makes a concerted effort to specifically define response times, a culture of urgency takes hold. Because team members feel they need to respond quickly or immediately, they allow notifications for their communication apps. And because some sort of communication comes in every minute or two, all team members are constantly distracted.

→ **Organization:** Team members ask each other for information necessary to get their jobs done. Information shared via these requests needs to be stored for potential later use in a way that is organized and accessible to others on the team. Without a system for organizing information, it can be difficult and time consuming for team members to access necessary information in the future.

Team members have some control over some of these issues in some communication channels. They can control their distraction level from email and company chat, but not the volume. Similarly, they can control how organized their email is and set an email schedule for themselves, but they have no control over the organization and timetable of chat.

Particularly in the case of email, the entire team is affected by the volume of the communication, but only each individual team member is affected by the (dis)organization of their own inbox—some team members are very efficient with email processing and storage, and some are very inefficient. Also, each individual team member can control whether they allow distractions in the form of visual or audible notifications, but this decision is often impacted by the perceived expectations of others. If a team member feels that others expect an immediate response, they may translate this into a belief that one is required, whether it's true or not.

Chat, on the other hand, negatively affects everyone on the team due to both its volume and its disorganization. The storage and organization of the messages are the responsibility of everyone who participates. Here too, each individual team member can control whether they allow distractions in the form of visual or audible notifications, but this decision is again impacted by the perceived expectations of others.

All of the components in this chapter preventing fires versus fighting fires, approaching work in a thoughtful, deliberate manner rather than a haphazard, reactive way, and making information self-serve have something in common: to improve efficiency in our new reality of remote and hybrid work, organizations need to make a deliberate shift away from synchronous (real-time) communication to asynchronous (delayed) communication. Throughout this book, including in this chapter, you'll come across ideas for how to shift communication from synchronous to asynchronous, including specific techniques in chapter 9.

Case Study: Twist

To reiterate, none of the inefficiencies described earlier are caused by any specific tool. Everything mentioned earlier can be true for any email client and any team communication tool. And a major cause of the inefficient habits identified previously is that leadership usually does not consider the most effective and efficient use of apps and software within the organization, and does not offer any guidance to the team. But I've also seen how some tools can actually promote inefficient communication habits, and some can encourage more effective habits.

My team and I have embraced a team communication tool called Twist (twistapp.com), which was designed for asynchronous communication, making it different from other chat tools.

Because we have a small team and we are focused on productivity and effectiveness, we were able to see very quickly that we needed to create specific guidelines about how we would use the tool to communicate. (This is true not only for

Twist but also for any chat tool, and it's a step most organizations skip.)

Let's look at how my team's habits for using Twist impact each of the areas of inefficient communication identified earlier—volume, distraction, and organization.

Volume: We use Twist messages in place of email whenever possible. This allows us to vastly decrease the amount of email we send. It may seem like a wash—email volume goes down but Twist communication goes up—but it turns out that because Twist allows our communication to be centralized and organized well, less communication is required.

Distraction: Twist can be configured as a synchronous (immediate) communication tool when necessary, but it was built intentionally as an asynchronous communication tool. Its default use is for information that does not require an immediate response. There are no notifications, and it is not necessary to know who is "online" and who isn't. (As discussed earlier in this chapter, when leaders take on the job of organizing workflows thoughtfully and deliberately, immediate communication is rarely necessary.) Twist, therefore, generally discourages a culture of immediacy, and it is designed to alleviate some or all of the distraction that digital communication can cause.

Organization: Twist is designed to organize information

in channels and threads, and it has a search feature. But it still suffers a bit from the same challenges as any other team communication tool—its organization is only as good as the habits of the people using it. It does have one advantage over other team communication platforms (like Slack and Teams) with its "inbox" feature. All unread messages appear in one place, but when you select a message, it appears in its proper thread, aligned with all prior information on that topic. And you can mark each new message as "done," which helps ensure that nothing is missed.

The specific instructions for using Twist have been thoroughly detailed and organized by the team at Doist, the company behind Twist, in their user documentation (twist.com/help), in their practical *Ambition & Balance* blog (blog.doist.com), and in their excellent remote work guides (twist.com/remote-work-guides).

Benefits of My Team's Deliberate Communication Habits

Our improved communication habits, supported by using Twist, have yielded a variety of benefits, including the following:

➔ **Efficient use of resources:** I have minimized the company's investment in outsourced support but maximized the value of this work. We either spend less on contractors or spend the same amount but get more done as a team. Also, our contractors can more accurately predict their work from us, allowing them to strike the right balance of their preferred client load and downtime.

→ **Effective asynchronous communication:** It's rare that any of us needs anyone else on the team "right now." So each of us can plan our days in the ways that are most productive and convenient for us, knowing that we are unlikely to be distracted by other team members needing something from us "urgently."

→ **Easy access to current and historical data:** We have documented history of our past projects, allowing us to reuse past processes and learn from past mistakes. This also tends to shorten our project timelines.

→ **Time savings:** From my experience with clients, it takes about two minutes on average to read and assess an email. Since our team has virtually eliminated internal email communication, the only messages I send and receive now are external. I've shifted some of the time I used to spend reading and responding to emails to reviewing Twist instead, but I spend much less time and can tackle the work in a much more organized manner. This is because all the information I need to make decisions and answer questions is typically contained in the same thread, making it immediately accessible.

→ **Better decisions:** Twist allows me to address all questions related to one project or issue at the same time instead of jumping from project to project. Having our communication more organized and less time-sensitive allows us to call on Kahneman's "system 2 thinking" more often, facilitating stress reduction and more considered, rational decisions.

Example: Doist Team

Doist is a fully remote (what it calls "remote-first") technology company specializing in productivity software. It was founded in 2007, and the company is privately held, with more than 20 million users and approximately 120 employees based in 30 different countries around the world. Doist's team has been remote-first since its inception and has never had a corporate headquarters.

Doist's operations provide an example of how the processes I describe in this chapter offer efficient operations that fuel growth—even in a fully distributed environment—where burnout challenges don't exist, and employees have an appropriate work-life balance and are happy and engaged at work. Chase Warrington, Doist's Head of Remote, told me that after a year of COVID lockdowns, Doist's engagement score based on a survey of its employees was 91 percent favorable.

The DO System for Project Management

Doist achieves an organized, coordinated approach to business by leveraging a project management system it created, called the DO (Doist objectives) system. It uses a combination of Doist's two products—Twist (the team communication tool) and Todoist (a task and project management tool)—plus Dropbox Paper for sharing documents. The goal is to promote transparency and accountability in the team's work.

Each month, they coordinate a series of DOs (projects), which are completed in four-week sprint cycles, beginning on the first Monday of the month and ending on the last Friday of the month. The DOs are completed by squads (cross-functional teams) and are led by a squad leader.

DOs begin as a thread (an asynchronous conversation on a very specific issue) in Twist, where someone proposes a project they want to tackle. As the idea is formulated through this asynchronous conversation, it's converted into a formal spec document in Dropbox Paper, which is then shared in a dedicated Twist channel (channels unite threads around broad topics like team, project, location, or area of interest). The spec document contains everything one would need to know about this DO, including the stakeholders, the measurable goals and expected outcomes, and the timeline for completion.

Every month, the leadership team decides which DOs they will prioritize and assigns teammates to their respective squads. Once the DO is ready to begin, it is added to a template in Dropbox Paper, which is shared with the company in Twist. Squad leaders then leverage Todoist to assign tasks to their squads and create a timeline. They use Twist to communicate and Todoist to assign tasks and take action. Whether the DO is completed or not, team members use a DO retrospective channel in Twist to report the outcome of the DO, and list any ongoing work and who the directly responsible Doister is in case any lingering conversations need to take place.

Intentionally deciding on what projects will be executed and creating transparent project specifications allows Doist teams to determine how many people they'll need for a given project and what the deliverables will be for those people. This information is visible to everyone in the organization, which allows them to measure workloads and make priorities clear. Being assigned to a DO may not take up 100 percent of an employee's time during a month, but it is the employee's top priority. This allows employees to make progress collectively and individually, and makes everyone's responsibilities and priorities clear and transparent.

Doist team members can move their work forward independently, without their work being held up by other people, so real-time communication is rarely necessary. They don't have to be tied to their email inbox or chat tools. In fact, they estimate that about 1 percent of their communication is done via email, and they have an expectation of delayed response times. Delays of more than a day are not uncommon, and this fact doesn't cause problems.

I interviewed Chase Warrington, head of remote for Doist, and he told me they have found that "if you eliminate [communication-based distractions] and just let people focus on their actual work, then it becomes super easy to accomplish a lot in a relatively short period of time."

How to Prevent Silos and Disconnect

Fully distributed teams, or fully remote employees, can pose the challenge of team members getting disconnected and isolated and departments becoming siloed. Leaders need to create space for socializing and connecting on nonwork topics. This space should show up in team communication channels, in meetings, and in team, department, and organization-wide retreats.

Consider whether your organization's version of remote work requires someone to be responsible for its vision and implementation. If this is a big part of your culture now or you expect it to be in the future, consider a "head of remote" position like the one Doist has created. If your team will be hybrid instead of fully distributed, perhaps a different title is more appropriate.

It's important to identify the responsibilities of this role. The primary responsibility would be to ensure that all team members are engaged and have what they need to be successful. This is not necessarily a traditional human resources role but could include the following responsibilities:

→ Executing, tracking, and analyzing "employee pulse" surveys. These are check-in type surveys that are typically short—in many cases just one question—but frequent, and they help leaders keep their finger on the pulse of the team. There are many tools that help with this execution, and most come with templates for these pulse surveys. These tools also make employee engagement easy to track over time.

→ Organizing all-company, on-site meetings and facilitating smaller, more frequent, regional connections.

→ Creating space for employees to connect beyond work, such as opening meetings with a check-in activity and designating one or more chat channels to things like jokes, vacation photos, life events, etc.

→ Reporting "internal public relations" to share communication regarding organizational events and initiatives, financial results, and other company news.

→ Facilitating cross-functional teams so employees from different teams have the chance to meet and work with others in the organization.

Implementing the suggestions in this chapter will provide a blueprint for continuous improvement of your organization or department. You'll reduce stress, reduce the volume of communication the team needs to manage daily, enable the team to be more thoughtful and engage in more system 2 thinking, create an opportunity for both the quality and the quantity of work to increase without an increase in working hours, and empower the team to dedicate more resources to their physical and emotional well-being, their families, and their communities.

3

Changing a Culture of Urgency

A more organized, coordinated approach to work goes a long way toward changing a culture of urgency, but expectations around email—especially customer email—can undermine your efforts. You'll need to examine habits exhibited by leadership, corporate systems, and company hardware to determine if your company practices and expectations support efficient, balanced, and productive use of email, or whether habits and assumptions have taken root that are sabotaging your employees' energy, effectiveness, and efficiency.

How Leaders Influence Communication

When leaders always expect an immediate response to their emails, they (perhaps inadvertently) tie employees to their inboxes. Even if you don't expect an immediate response, do your employees think you do? Or do they think you will look more favorably on an immediate response? When companies fall into the habit of using internal email for immediate and urgent communication, the (often unintended) by-product is that employees are forced to always leave their email open, so they're distracted by every new message that comes in.

> **A reactive work culture means important work takes a back seat to immediate demands.**

Having a culture of urgency puts employees in reactive mode all day and prevents them from being proactive. They aren't assessing their overall workload and choosing what to work on next. Important work takes a back seat to immediate demands. This kind of culture also creates constant multi-tasking (task switching) and prevents employees from ever being able to focus on the task at hand for any period of time. Study after study shows that task switching causes work to both take longer and be of lower quality.[i] I often hear from clients that they find it difficult even to begin a larger task because they anticipate interruptions and therefore feel discouraged from even getting started.

Manage Your Technology

In most email clients, the messages arrive without invitation by the user. You can employ a variety of solutions to give you and your team members more control over whether you receive email or not.

In addition to turning off the notifications, which should be encouraged at your company (even set as the default by the IT department), you can also encourage the team to work in offline mode. (In Microsoft Outlook, this can usually be found on the Send/Receive ribbon.) This means that messages you send will not be delivered until you disable offline mode, but the productivity gains of offline mode far outweigh the slight delay of sending messages.

Another option is "inbox pause," a service offered for Outlook, Gmail, and iPhones (www.inboxpause.com). Of course, closing out email is the easiest solution, but often the work you do requires information currently being stored in your inbox.

ELIMINATE INAPPROPRIATE HARDWARE

· ·

Rethink company support for the two (or more) computer monitors discussed in the Designed for Distraction section in chapter 1. Providing multiple monitors not only condones constant distraction but also actually encourages it. Offer extra monitors to those whose jobs will benefit from them—like designers, architects, and finance professionals—but ask others to think about how they plan to use a second monitor, and whether this will support or sabotage thoughtful work.

Unintentional Email Habits

There is an argument to be made that email changed the very nature of "real work" but in an unstructured, inefficient way rather than an intentional, thoughtful way. Our use of email and our expectations around it are certainly among the "unconscious calculations" I mentioned in the introduction.

Computer science professor and author Cal Newport

wrote in the *Harvard Business Review* that "It's important to remember that no blue ribbon committee or brilliant executive ever sat down and decided that this workflow [email] would make businesses more productive or employees more satisfied. It instead just emerged as an instinctual reaction to a disruptive new technology."[ii] Thoughtfully planning work in a more strategic way can at first be harder than an unstructured, ad hoc approach, but it's also more efficient.

It's time to make intentional decisions about our use of email and all other communication tools. The work I proposed in the earlier sections will initially be difficult to implement, but the returns can be exponential.

4

Fast Doesn't Equal Better

After reading about the argument I made for asynchronous communication earlier in the book, you might be thinking that this isn't possible in your organization because it will have a negative impact on your clients. Part of the difficulty of reversing a culture of immediacy is that we have allowed speed of response time to become a customer service metric. This is another of the "unconscious calculations" I mentioned in the introduction. Most leaders seem to believe that good customer service involves being "responsive" or offering "timely" responses to requests. They apply this belief to external customers but often to internal customers as well. But the cost of that approach to customer service is far too high. And is speed really the metric on which you want to evaluate your team or your organization?

Speed can be imitated, and it's finite. It's not really a competitive advantage, because others can easily adopt the same strategy (and probably do). And pretty soon, everyone in your organization is living in chaos trying to respond to every communication immediately, which can't really be done, and the effort is burning out your team, making them busy but unproductive, and preventing them from doing thoughtful, satisfying work. Quality is a better differentiator, and a better metric of success.

Speed of Response Times as an Unconscious Calculation

The idea that lightning-quick responses to incoming emails are necessary is typically conveyed by leadership as an obvious fact, with no thought or explanation about what it means for the bigger picture. I see it translated in my client companies this way:

→ Responsive = fast

→ If fast is good, then immediate must be best.

→ Most corporate communication is done via email, and therefore to excel at customer service, I should respond immediately to emails.

> **A fast response doesn't always mean your team or company is being responsive— it just means you're fast.**

This translation is often done unconsciously. It's not discussed. It's just a group assumption that happens without intention. Immediate email responses lead to expectations of immediate responses to all types of communication, such as texts and messages in team collaboration tools, like Slack and Teams.

A fast response doesn't always mean your team or company is being responsive—it just means you're fast. And fast replies often lack appropriate consideration, contain mistakes, and increase stress in team members.

The result is a culture of urgency. If your company has adopted these assumptions, the expected email response time in your workplace is probably "the sooner, the better." And that expectation is devastating to knowledge worker productivity.

Synchronous email communication might feel productive, because every message addressed feels like one less thing you have to do—an imaginary check off your mental to-do list. But email as real-time communication creates unrealistic expectations, because no one can ever answer all emails they receive in real time. Far from being productive, the futile pursuit of synchronous email communication squeezes out the more important work that really provides not only good customer service, but also organizational success. Think about it: no one at your company was hired for how fast they answer emails.

The Difference between "Fast" and "Responsive"

Because this use of speed as a success metric happens organically, without intention, it's implemented without consideration to the fact that good (responsive) customer service should also mean the following:

→   providing the right information in the most helpful way

→   doing work thoughtfully, creatively, and accurately

→   solving problems

→   being empathetic with clients and colleagues

→   recognizing insights gained from customer interactions and applying them to improve product and service offerings

→   being present with customers and actively listening to their needs

With this in mind, you shouldn't require employees to reply to messages as fast as possible. It is better for them to acquire the information they need and think through the most effective way to communicate what it is they'd like to say.

Maybe you're thinking that you'll tell your team they don't need to respond to every communication immediately, only those from customers or prospects. But this doesn't work, because what is distracting and stressing your team is not necessarily responding to the messages, it's the constant checking to see which messages are from clients and which aren't.

The components of responsive customer service are all the result of thoughtful attention to communication. Responding to every message as it arrives (or just checking to see if that new message requires an immediate response) means busy professionals spend a lot of time switching between their important work and monitoring their email. This virtually guarantees that your team members are rarely or never devoting sustained attention to the important knowledge work you hired them for, the thoughtful service that will make your customers happy, and that will power your organization's success—such as analysis, creativity, problem-solving, relationship building, and innovation.

Treating email as a synchronous communication tool

means your organization isn't leveraging its people. It also reinforces a culture of urgency, because the more senders receive an immediate response, the more they expect an immediate response.

For employees to be productive, your organization needs a clear communication policy that includes response-time expectations. Leaders need to be intentional and specific about how email should be handled and how to balance responsiveness with thoughtful work time. And leadership needs to model the desired behaviors.

A Thoughtful Approach to Communication

To be effective, your policy first needs to provide guidance for how to match the medium to the message. For example, many situations are not appropriate for email communication, such as urgent, time-sensitive, and emotionally charged matters. Information on shared projects is also more appropriate for team collaboration tools instead of email, as discussed in chapter 2.

Next, your policy should take different job roles into consideration. The customer service team probably needs to be more responsive than the C-level executives. But those team members who are responsible for receiving customer issues and complaints still need time away from receiving these issues in order to thoughtfully solve them.

You might be thinking that being thoughtful and deliberate about communications sounds nice but would never work for your business. You might think that getting back to clients right away is essential to keeping them, or that if you don't return a call or text from a prospect immediately, they'll just move on to another provider.

In my experience, these are outdated fears that no longer hold true in our digital age. At the very least, I suggest you test this assumption with data to determine if it's really true. It might be another unconscious calculation.

Reputation Capital

For once, here's some good news about the state of the world: it's less competitive than it used to be.

Thirty years ago, when we wanted to buy a new product or service, we would look in the phone book. We would make a call, and if the phone wasn't answered or the call wasn't returned right away, we'd move on to the next name in the directory, because the only thing we knew about the company we called was the size of their ad in the yellow pages.

But the world isn't like that anymore. Today, thanks to the internet, consumers are able to do much more research into the companies we want to hire and the products we want to purchase. We review the company website, make comparisons between similar companies or products, ask for referrals from our social networks, and check the business's reputation or the product reviews on review sites.

These days, once a potential customer contacts you, they've already invested time and thought into the process, and they chose you, your organization, or someone on your team. Because of this investment and your reputation that caused them to reach out in the first place, they are much more likely to wait a reasonable amount of time before moving on.

This means that you have "reputation capital" that you can use to help employees focus better on their work and offer more thoughtful interactions with customers.

When you allow your employees to bring their best selves to their communications, they are going to deliver outstanding customer interactions. This will serve to further build your reputation capital. And equally important, when your team members know they are doing their best work, they will feel more productive and satisfied at the end of their workdays, be more engaged in their work, and be less likely to burn out.

I'm not suggesting you make clients or prospects wait days to hear from someone. In most cases, no later than the next business day is reasonable, as long as you set expectations properly through automation, and give existing clients a path in case of emergency. And your messaging in voicemail, email auto-responders, and other client communication channels is important in setting those expectations.

For example, proper expectations, instructions in case of emergency, and automation might look something like a voice-mail message or email auto-responder that offers language like, "Thank you so much for your inquiry! We're excited to serve you in the thoughtful, quality manner in which we serve all our clients. You can expect to hear from someone within one business day. However, if your message requires a more timely response, please feel free to text our emergency line at XXX-XXXX." Then give due consideration to the process you create to handle those "emergency" communications.

Reinvesting Your Reputation Capital to Improve Profitability

Just as you might reinvest income in your business, you need to do the same with the reputation capital you've earned—or else you're just squandering it. Specifically, I recommend you spend your reputation capital in ways that provide quality service to your clients and help team members feel energized and not depleted by their work.

The best way to use your hard-earned reputation capital

is by applying it to reduce distraction and pull back from a culture of urgency that is creating stress and pressure for your team. Instead, invest in a culture that puts an emphasis on attention management. Here's what that might look like:

→ You encourage team members to provide the most thoughtful, helpful responses to customers and colleagues, and you reduce the pressure they feel to respond to incoming messages as soon as possible.

→ You and other company leaders model work-life balance. You regularly take time off and don't communicate with team members after hours unless there's a true emergency.

→ You encourage employees to engage in deep, focused work so they can offer their best in the service of your organization's success.

When you build a company culture that prioritizes attention management, you get happier employees, more satisfied customers, and a more robust bottom line. So a culture of attention management is also a great way to *create* reputation capital.

Serving Internal Customers

For team members who don't provide direct service to customers, your communication policy needs to provide "breathing room." A useful technique can be to have employees add a line to their email signatures that reads something like, "Thoughtful work time is important to our success. Therefore, I only check email periodically throughout the day. If your message is of a more urgent or timely nature, please feel free to…" (This will be different depending on the role, but it could read "open a support ticket," or "call the receptionist and ask them to find me," or "call the 800 number," for example.)

Employees whose most important job outcomes include creativity and critical thinking need more leeway in their communication practices. This includes senior leadership, those in creative roles, and those in detail-oriented roles, like programmers, finance team members, and analysts. When they can be less distracted by email, they will have more opportunity for the sustained, focused time required to do the deep thinking, creative, and visionary work they were hired to do.

When your organization implements an intentional email response-time policy that thoughtfully considers what good customer service really means, you'll create a culture that supports your team's ability to do their best work. It will help them overcome their habit of distraction, improve their attention spans and patience, and engage their "brainpower momentum" in support of high-level knowledge work. In addition, they'll feel a greater sense of satisfaction and meaning because their days will hold more satisfying accomplishments than the busywork of email.

Isn't all that worth waiting a little longer for a response to your message?

5

A Leadership Formula to Empower Teams

One of the reasons leaders tell me they feel they can't escape getting distracted by their team members is because they consider addressing these distractions to be an important part of their jobs. They want to be available to make decisions and mentor their staff through problems. They tell me, "My team is always interrupting me with questions and issues, and I need to be available so they can move their work forward and I don't become the bottleneck in the process."

Everyone likes to feel important and needed, and being available to your team can seem like a primary role of a manager, so it can be hard to recognize this as a problem. But in order to be agile and adaptable, companies need team members who are empowered to creatively and independently solve problems.

To create the reflective thinking time your organization needs from you, you need to facilitate your team members' independence. This is especially important if your team is not physically together, because "quick questions" sent through team chat channels can otherwise be endless.

To empower your team, start by analyzing the problem. What are the reasons your team members feel they need your input? Is it because they don't have the confidence to make decisions on their own? Because they fear reprisals if they make the "wrong" decision? Because they are unqualified or inexperienced? Categorizing the types of issues can help you recognize patterns and take corrective action.

Once you understand what your direct reports are coming to you about, then you need to determine why, and what role you play in that. Does your behavior enable or even encourage your staff to bring you every little "speed bump" in their day? Does it lead them to believe that you are the only one who is authorized to solve problems or make decisions? Does the way you interact with them cause them to lack confidence in their own judgment or make the limits of their authority unclear to them? Do they have good reason to fear making a mistake?

In chapter 2, I made an argument about why allowing

these distractions and getting involved in day-to-day problems isn't the best use of a leader's time. In this chapter, I'll offer several suggestions for how to manage less and lead more, allowing you to spend more time on the business rather than in it.

Create Boundaries for Decision-Making

Sometimes, it's hard for employees to determine what they should handle on their own and what is outside the scope of their responsibilities. Ensure that each of your team members knows exactly what their ultimate role in the company is, and when it's acceptable for them to make mistakes within that role. They need to understand which decisions fall within the scope of their responsibilities and which decisions are outside that scope. This helps them understand the consequences of their actions, take ownership of their job, and be accountable.

An added benefit of this clarity is creative thinking in unusual circumstances that can't be predicted. For example, the customer service staff at online retailer Zappos know that their ultimate role is "to create a what they call a WOW experience for their customers," and when they make decisions based on that motivation, they'll be praised and not scolded. The freedom to accomplish this goal as they see fit unleashes their creativity. For example, one Zappos customer service representative sent flowers to cheer up a customer who shared on a call that they were having a bad day. Another customer service representative reportedly researched local pizza restaurants to assist a customer who mentioned they were hungry. Employees didn't need permission to go above and beyond in these ways, even when spending company funds was involved. This level of creative and unrestricted customer service also leads to free positive press, loyal customers, and organizational success.

Be Available Less Often

Think of those times when you've been working but away from your email for extended periods, like while you are attending an off-site meeting or conference. When you got back to it, have you ever seen a series of emails from one or more members of your team in a progression similar to the following?

→ **Oldest message:** "Hey, boss, I know you're out of the office today, but we're having this issue we'd like to discuss with you…"

→ **Next message:** "I guess you're still tied up, but if you can squeeze in a minute to call the office…"

→ **Last message:** "Never mind. We figured it out."

The lesson here is that if the boss is unavailable more

often, the team figures things out on their own more often. This allows them to grow in their positions, and it minimizes the interruptions the leaders face.

This situation illuminates other problems (besides distraction) that arise when leaders are "too available" to the team. For example, when staff constantly bring questions and problems to the boss and the boss provides answers and solutions, this can create the unintentional consequence of the team becoming disempowered (or lazy). It can promote the idea that the boss is available to help team members overcome every little speed bump in their day, and it reinforces the behavior loop of "questions/problems arise; I bring them to my boss; my boss provides answers/solutions." This dynamic pushes too many decisions to the top and creates speed bumps and bottlenecks that are obstacles to innovation.

If, instead, the boss rebuffs the interruption with some variation of the phrase, "I trust your judgment," then the team will feel empowered and will grow in their positions—and ultimately interrupt the boss less. This is especially true when team members are clear in the scope of their responsibilities. When you encourage your team members to find their own solutions to day-to-day problems by using the phrase "I trust your judgment," they will become more confident with every problem they solve on their own.

> **Refrain from saying to the team, "Don't come to me with problems, come to me with solutions." Because if they know the problem and they know the solution, there is no need for them to come to you!**

When I'm delivering a leadership workshop and I share this information, someone in the audience invariably interjects, "I think you're right. That's why I tell my team, 'Don't come to me with problems. Come to me with solutions!'" That's a good start, but if your staff has identified a problem and has the solution, why do they need to come to you at all? Let them deal with the issue on their own, and then "mentor in hindsight," which I'll discuss soon.

Avoid Micromanaging

What if you don't trust a team member's judgment? If this is the case, you first have to determine whether the problem is really with the employee's judgment or whether the real issue is that you are the kind of manager who likes having a lot of control and being involved in every decision. This kind of micromanaging is a burden on you and stifles your team's growth. You can't do everyone's job for them, nor should you. Empower your team members to make their own decisions. If you are unsure whether you are micromanaging, ask a trusted peer or former employee to give you honest feedback.

If you learn that you are micromanaging, I recommend that you seek out leadership development opportunities for yourself, as this management style can be toxic and even dangerous to your team members, especially if their jobs are demanding. A study published in *Personnel Psychology* found that in jobs where employees felt they had low levels of control, the employees' odds of dying were higher than in jobs where they felt they had more control.[i]

Embrace the Tough Decisions

If you determine that you aren't micromanaging but there are employees whose judgment you don't trust, try to understand why, so you can find remedies. Do the employees have a gap in their skills? Help them get training to fill it. If it's a common problem on the team, bring training in-house. If it's an isolated issue, task the employee to find outside or online training on the topic. At the very least, recommend a book.

Is the person new to the organization? Perhaps more time is needed to learn the ropes. Maybe finding a mentor or "buddy" on the team would be helpful—ideally someone besides you. But put boundaries around this ramp-up time. When onboarding new employees, provide a road map and timeline for getting up to speed. For example, "For the first week of your job, you can take as much of my time as you need and ask me anything. In the second week, we'll meet twice a week for an hour. In week three, we'll drop to one sixty-minute meeting, and in week four, I expect you to be able to handle most things on your own, and we'll adopt the same meeting schedule I have with the rest of my direct reports." Make sure they also get dedicated training—separate from this time with you—on any organizational software that is unfamiliar.

Occasionally, you may find you've made a hiring mistake. The hardest questions to face are whether you have the right person in the wrong role, or whether the person isn't a good fit for the organization. Don't drag your feet here. Make it a win for you and for the employee by helping the person find another role at your organization, or a new job somewhere else. This will enable you to cut your losses as well as help develop your company's reputation as a good place to work.

Hold Regular One-on-One Meetings

In my experience with clients, I've found that the common ways of using one-on-one meetings are not the most effective. Typical agendas for meetings between a manager and a direct report include the following:

→ status updates
→ collective decision-making
→ joint problem-solving
→ seeking/granting permission for specific activities or courses of action

In chapter 2, I discussed making information "self-serve" through effective use of project management and team communication tools. When implemented successfully, you won't need to get in-person (synchronous) status updates from team members, because that information will be accessible to you (asynchronously) any time.

If you follow the advice in this chapter for empowering your team members, you won't need to use the time to help them make decisions or solve problems, and they won't feel the need to ask your permission for things.

Instead, make your one-on-one meetings with your direct reports shorter and more effective by shifting the agenda.

With some strategic questions, you can use the time in the following ways instead:

→ learning about how they handle their work, make decisions, and think critically

→ celebrating their wins and offering praise and recognition

→ holding them accountable for mistakes but in an empathetic way

→ being a mentor and helping them learn and grow

→ helping them take away the lessons from their experiences

Your specific questions can vary based on the person and the situation, of course, but these three types of questions can uncover the information in the above points:

 What kinds of challenges did you face/problems did you encounter this week?

 What did you do to overcome/solve them?

 How did that go?

Open your meetings with succinct questions like these, and then be silent. You may be surprised at how much you

learn through your own silence and active listening. Your employees are very likely to fill the silence.

There is one characteristic of your culture that is necessary for all the advice in this chapter to be relevant: your direct reports and department—ideally, the organization's entire team—must believe that they are in an environment where it is safe to make mistakes.

Create a Safe Environment to Make Mistakes

By "mistakes," I don't mean errors that result from carelessness or not following policies. I mean good faith attempts to overcome a challenge that just didn't work out well. When you ask the previous questions in your one-on-one meetings, your employees will only be honest if they feel safe doing so. If there are serious, unpleasant consequences for making honest mistakes, your organization has a "CYA culture" instead of a culture of accountability. People aren't coming to you because they truly value your input; they're just looking for a way to shift any future blame. So anytime something goes wrong, they can say, "It's not my fault. You said I could do it." This pervasive unaccountability will stifle growth, disempower your team, create bottlenecks, and prevent your organization from being adaptable.

If you want innovative team members who work independently, they will inevitably try something that doesn't work out, and may have negative consequences. But with the right leadership, the consequences of mistakes is much smaller than the benefits received by having an agile, creative, empowered team.

Hold team members accountable for their decisions in an empathetic way by using mistakes as teaching opportunities. Take the advice of leadership expert and bestselling author John C. Maxwell from his book of the same name, *Sometimes You Win, Sometimes You Learn*. Ask them specifically what they learned from the experience. Then underscore the lesson and make sure it sticks, but if the decision was ethical and made in good faith, be supportive. This is often referred to as "psychological safety." Give team members the benefit of the doubt unless and until they prove they don't deserve it.

Other factors that contribute to team member satisfaction and psychological safety include trust, recognition, having input, and feeling heard. When team members have successes, celebrate with them, and recognize their successes publicly whenever possible. David Hassell, CEO of performance management software company 15five, offers a great list of additional questions for your one-on-one meetings:[ii]

→ What can I do to help you be more successful?

→ How are you feeling at work lately? How's the morale around you?

→ On a scale of 1–10, how satisfied are you? Why?

→ What's the best thing that happened to you this week, either at work or outside it?

→ If you had the chance, what's one thing you would do to improve the product or service provided by our company?

→ If you owned the company, what's one thing you would do differently?

→ What were some great contributions made by other team members recently?

→ What can I do to be a better leader?

Psychological safety maintains your team members' motivation to try new things. I believe people live up to our expectations of them, and in my experience, this is especially true of leaders who are respected, liked, and admired by their direct reports. If your team members feel that way about you, they won't want to disappoint you.

Mentor in Hindsight

The last agenda item for one-on-one meetings that empower and motivate your team is what I call "mentoring in hindsight."

Mentoring is an important role of leadership and helps groom employees to advance within the organization. However, they learn much less when advice is given on the front end than they do when they have the opportunity to experience their own successes and failures and discuss them with you later.

So after you've heard from your team members about their challenges and their successes, and you've celebrated their wins and helped them take the lessons from their mistakes, then and only then is it time for you to offer them the benefit of your opinions and experience by sharing your ideas of what you would have done in the situations they discuss with you (if your ideas differ from what they did).

People learn more by doing than by being told what to do, so this provides them the best of both worlds: they learned from their own experiences (good and bad), and then you offer them another tool for their toolbox or another approach to try in a future, similar situation. Better than offering mentoring in *advance* of a situation is mentoring in hindsight.

6

Take Vacation Seriously

In my work with leaders and teams, I'm struck by how pervasive the erosion of actual vacation has become. A common refrain I heard during the pandemic that frankly left me speechless was "I'm not taking any vacation time because there's nothing to do besides work."

To me, this illustrates how much we have lost our way with regard to the importance of downtime and its relationship to burnout, physical and emotional well-being, creativity, and motivation.

An overlooked fact about vacation is the return on investment. If you offer your employees paid vacation, the company is making an investment in their opportunity to recharge, refresh, and refocus. If team members are available for work issues when on vacation, they aren't really getting the benefits they're being paid to receive, and the organization is not receiving any return on its investment. A vacation allows you distance from your work and your everyday life that provides a new perspective, creativity boost, and clarity of thought that gets buried by the fast pace and regularity of your daily routine. With new perspective comes new insight. Think about it this way: you can't get a fresh perspective on something you never step away from.

Studies show that time away from work provides many physical and mental health benefits, including lowering the risk of heart attacks, anxiety, and depression.[i] And remember: physical and emotional well-being are the grease and the gas that allow the machinery of knowledge work to operate. The most important tool of knowledge work is the brain, and overworking degrades the performance of that tool.

Paradoxically, one of the biggest reasons that people resist taking time off—because they think their work or their career will suffer if they do—has been debunked by a wealth of research over the last decade. Productivity and job satisfaction have been shown to increase with time off, but there is also evidence that people who take vacation time can increase their odds of raises and promotions.[ii]

Defining Terms Related to Downtime

Vacation is one of the many words that are critical to explicitly define for your team. Not only *vacation* but other words related to time other than working time, such as *workweek, paid time off, emergencies,* and *downtime* also need to be explicitly defined.

I often tell my leadership clients and their team members that the best thing they can do *for* their work is work less. This is because the downtime our brains need to be inspired and innovative is usually undervalued in the service of more work. Daydreaming, resting, and doing other things all help restore motivation and creativity.

But with the expansion of working from home and the resulting flextime (which has really become "always on"), most knowledge workers never have the opportunity to fully disconnect. This seriously undermines productivity.

Workweek

First, be explicit about your expectations of your team members. Is it hours or outcomes, or both? For example, if it's a common belief of your employees that fifty-plus-hour weeks are required, does that align with your company values and your leadership beliefs? Contribute to being intentional about the way the organization is being run and whether assumed or unstated beliefs are undermining your culture.

Strictly results-based work environments are less common, harder to implement and manage, and outside the scope of this book. So if you don't already have one, it will be easier to start with an expectation of hours worked.

So the first term to explicitly define is *workweek*. By clearly defining when employees should and shouldn't be routinely available—establishing business hours or expected workweek durations—you'll help them unplug on a regular basis. As a result, they'll be much better able to apply their focused attention at work. Going forward, however, it may be that different employees on the same team keep different work hours from each other.

But just because an employee is on the clock at a certain time doesn't mean that others have to be, and making clear what you expect from a typical workweek is critical (forty-five hours? fifty? fifty-five? Studies show that productivity takes a serious dip after fifty-five hours per week).[iii] This should also be considered an average, as work volume often varies.

Vacation/Paid Time Off (PTO)

A vacation renews perspective and clarity of thought that gets buried by the fast pace of everyday life. Research from Project: Time Off actually shows that people who take vacation are more likely to get promoted and get a raise.[iv] Not bad.

Unfortunately, American workers are less likely to take vacation than ever before; they believe doing so will negatively affect their reputations. And workers in companies with unlimited vacation policies often feel even more pressure to show their commitment to their jobs.

> **Specifically define vacation at your company in a way that allows your team to have a crystal-clear understanding of what you expect when they're away—absolutely nothing.**

But for vacation time to truly work its magic—happier employees while away, increased productivity and revenues upon return—the vacation has to be a time of true disconnection from the office. Employees who check email "only" once a day still won't reap the benefits of a fully unplugged vacation; they'll lie on the beach anxiously running through all the tasks they aren't doing at work. There is an important difference between "working while traveling" and "vacation." The former is work time. The latter most decidedly is not.

Specifically define vacation at your company in a way that allows your team to have a crystal-clear understanding of what you expect when they're away—absolutely nothing. And model a vacation-friendly culture by ensuring the leaders don't head out with instructions like, "I'm off to Aruba with the family, but feel free to call me if you need me." This will undermine your message about the importance of vacation, make your leaders look like hypocrites, and erode the trust in your culture.

Your initial thoughts about this idea might be that it's relevant for some of your staff but not all (like leadership). This is a mistake. The benefits of vacation are true for everyone. If there are any people in your organization you feel are absolutely critical to operations all the time and can never be out of touch, then you're not empowering and growing your team, you're not cultivating an appropriate succession plan, and the organization is at serious risk if something should prevent that central person from continuing to do their job. And it may be that this person is at greater risk of a burnout-related absence, so the organization is at risk in two ways: it can't function without that person, and that fact creates added stress on that person which increases their risk of being absent.

You'll never know how and if the organization can function without certain individuals if those individuals are never out of touch. Insisting that everyone takes time away and that they don't work when they're gone is a good initial test, and will also support more efficient operations and succession planning moving forward. This is in addition to the increase in creativity, motivation, and inspiration provided by the vacation that will benefit both the individual and the organization.

Emergency

A common refrain is that no one should "bother" someone on vacation "unless it's an emergency." Or a staffer departing from the office might say, "Call me if there is an emergency." You'll need to define what constitutes an "emergency" in advance, and it may be different for every job role. There are likely some staffers for whom there is no situation that would require their assistance while they are out. Often, defining emergencies is the first step in contingency planning for an organization, which can be a very helpful exercise.

Creating a Vacation-Friendly Culture

The U.S. Travel Association's State of American Vacation Report from 2018, the last year that data was available, showed that 52 percent of employees forfeited some of their vacation time (sometimes referred to as "work martyrdom"), and the following were the top reasons:

→ fear of looking replaceable

→ thinking their workload was too heavy for them to take time off

→ having no coverage or feeling that no one else can do their job[v]

What I often hear from my clients is something like, *"Why take a vacation at all? What's the point when I have to check email from the beach just to keep up with the constant stream of work and avoid a massive backlog when I return?"* In other words, workers feel the need to be "always on" to keep up with workplace demands. This was true before the pandemic, but is exponentially more of a problem postpandemic as we struggle with new work environments that involve much more working from home.

Since team members often struggle with the idea of taking vacation time, leaders need to create a vacation-friendly culture in order to reap the rewards and gain the competitive advantage of a creative, motivated workforce.

Leaders Must Model Healthy Behaviors

When it comes to work-life balance and time-off behavior, leaders wield an outsized influence. If you (or your team members) work incessantly and meet your professional goals, but you've done so at the expense of your personal life, your family, or your mental or physical health, is that the kind of "success" you aspire to? And is that what you want for your employees? Even if you believe that your employees' single-minded focus on work will help you achieve your department or company goals, I hope this book is beginning to convince you this is a misguided perspective. In the short term, your employees are likely not offering their best work, and the detriments will become more apparent over time in employee burnout, turnover, difficulty in recruiting the best people, and the erosion of a positive work culture.

Research done by the Energy Project in conjunction with *Harvard Business Review* of nineteen thousand employees around the world, resulted in the following conclusion:

> When leaders model in their own behavior sustainable ways of working, the effect on those they lead is far bigger. Unfortunately, only 25 percent of our survey respondents told us that their leaders model

sustainable work practices. Those leaders' employees are 55 percent more engaged, 72 percent higher in health and well-being, 77 percent more satisfied at work, and 1.15 times more likely to stay at the company. They also reported more than twice the level of trust in their leaders.[vi]

For companies to reap the benefits of their investment in vacation time for their employees, the solution has to be more comprehensive than simply adjusting to a new policy like "unlimited" vacation time. It's not sufficient to just state that employees need to take time away from work to restore. Company leaders must do more than talk.

I often hear leaders say that they hold themselves to higher work standards than they expect from their employees. But this too is a misguided perspective. First, you benefit from downtime the same way your team members do. Second, you can't create a vacation-friendly culture if you don't model the behaviors. If you won't take time off for your own good, think about doing it for the well-being of your employees.

How to Show Support for Time Off

If you think you have a neutral stance on vacation time by neither vocally encouraging it nor discouraging it, employees are likely to interpret your silence on the topic as meaning you implicitly discourage time off. Likewise, if you reach out by phone or email to an employee who's on vacation, you're communicating an expectation that they should work during their time off—even if you argue that they "should know" that you don't expect a reply until they're back at work.

Here are other ways that leaders can show support for time off, help employees feel good about taking time to recharge, and reap the benefits of increased productivity and fresh creativity inside the organization:

→ **Engage in a frank discussion with your leadership team about what managers and executives truly believe about time off.** Do they discourage, even inadvertently, using vacation days or fully unplugging while on vacation? Some on your leadership team (maybe you?) may need to be convinced of the benefit of sustainable work practices. Once you achieve buy-in around this belief in the well-being of your employees, ensure that your workplace culture, leadership behaviors, and employee assumptions are in line with those beliefs.

→ **Use your own paid time off, and don't check in with the office.** This means not reading your email (not just refraining from responding to email) while you're on vacation.

You'll get all the restorative benefits of vacation yourself, of course, and you'll be modeling healthy behavior for employees. Encourage everyone, especially the leaders and influencers at your organization, to do the same.

→ **Clearly communicate your support for taking paid time off and being fully away from work during vacations.** In today's work environment, failing to encourage vacation time (or failing to support unplugging) is awfully close to actually discouraging vacation time.

→ **Help employees acquire workflow management skills and tools.** Most knowledge workers, despite the levels of career success they have achieved, don't have the skills to manage their responsibilities most efficiently. (Workflow management skills are the focus of my prior books, *Personal Productivity Secrets* and the three books in the Empowered Productivity series.) These skills facilitate their ability to set boundaries, better understand priorities and deadlines, and protect their vacation time. Workflow management skills aren't taught in school, and as technology and communication channels proliferate, managing work effectively and efficiently is getting harder and harder.

→ **Implement a policy that a manager going on vacation can choose a trusted staffer to take on *all* of that manager's responsibilities.** This provides incentive to the manager to avoid checking in, because that would be perceived as a lack of confidence in the staffer. Additionally, the staff person has an opportunity to learn, grow, and be groomed for advancement. (One of my clients told me that this "boss for a day/week" was a common practice at IBM in the 1980s, designed to support the "promote from within" culture famous at IBM.)

Harnessing Technology in Support of Vacation

In addition to showing support and modeling the benefits of disconnecting during vacations, technology solutions and innovative polices are another option. For example, it's easy to temporarily hide or disable work email on a smartphone. This can help you resist the temptation to check in, and everyone in the organization should know how to do it and be reminded to do it when they are heading out for vacation time.

Enlist your IT staff to help your employees renew and recharge during their downtime instead of being tied to their email. For example, the IT team can show all staff how to schedule outgoing mail so that people can write messages whenever they like, but those messages will only get sent during business hours or when a colleague has returned from vacation. Additionally, the IT team should teach all staff how to put an out-of-office message on their email, voicemail, and chat tools.

Vacation tip: since it's often so hectic when employees are preparing to be out on vacation, I recommend encouraging team members (and leaders) to add the vacation message to email and voicemail one day before actual departure and leave it there until at least one day after return. This makes it easier for employees to transition to being off and to have time to catch up upon return.

To take your policy even further, your IT staff could change vacationing staffers' email and voicemail passwords (or restrict access in other ways) so they can't retrieve messages while on vacation, even if they want to.

This section has detailed several ways to show support for vacation and help employees physically disconnect. Still, it's important to recognize that these solutions don't fully address the anxiety a staffer might have at the prospect of being away or of returning to a mountain of work. Knowing their boss fully supports their disconnected time will help. And the next sections will offer other suggestions for alleviating the anxiety.

Reducing Out-of-Office Anxiety

An increasing number of organizations are taking vacation so seriously that they have adopted policies that you might consider radical at first glance. But if I've convinced you of the benefits of vacation and other downtime, especially for knowledge workers, then the return on the investment in vacation should be an incentive to experiment with new policies.

One way to alleviate your team's anxiety about the work that's piling up in their inboxes while they're away is to model a policy that gained widespread attention for Mercedes-Benz (formerly Daimler) in 2014 and has since been adopted by other organizations. Mercedes-Benz calls it "Mail on Holiday," and it offers employees an opportunity to have their messages deleted while they are away, using an automated message similar to this one:

"Thank you for your message. I am on vacation, so please direct your communication to XX in my absence, or resend it after XX date when I will be back in the office. Your initial message has been deleted in my absence."

When I mention this option to leaders, their initial response is dismissal because they believe it would upset customers. For your industry or your business, that *may* be true. However, before immediately dismissing the idea, I suggest you consider ways to implement the policy that wouldn't be upsetting.

The first is to ask, is it true that customers would be upset? Another possible perspective is that the sender could be supportive of the vacationing staffer: "Good for Doreen, she deserves a vacation." Or they may even be envious of the policy: "How cool that she can delete her emails while on vacation!" This can result in your organization being seen as a great place to work.

If you have evidence that this policy would upset customers, is there a way to implement it *without* upsetting customers? Regardless of a specific employee's vacation status, it's useful to teach your customers how to interact with your organization in the most productive way. In chapter 9, I'll discuss communication guidelines, how to use them, and why they are useful. In addition to internal staff, it's also possible to train customers on your communication guidelines. Reinforce with customers the idea that email shouldn't be used in the case of time-sensitive or urgent communication, and provide an appropriate alternative (perhaps a phone number that is answered by a service that can route the call appropriately).

My point is not to dismiss out of hand the idea of diverting messages sent to a vacationing staffer. Question your assumptions, and consider how you could make it work.

While it's true that it's harder and takes more effort to be so deliberate with your policy, it's also likely to pay exponential dividends.

Another policy worthy of consideration is the one employed by CEO of Acceleration Partners Robert Glazer. Acceleration Partners offers a financial incentive of up to $750 for team members to fully unplug while on vacation. Glazer writes, "We don't want vacationing employees to glance at email or even send a Slack message."[vii] He says that in addition to the health benefits to the individual and the morale and engagement benefits to the organization, it also helps people learn to delegate, which contributes to a culture of high trust. According to Glazer, about 60 percent of its employees took advantage of the program in 2019.

Unlimited Time Off

Implementing the practices in this chapter might solve some or all of the vacation problems at your organization, but you might also be interested in a recent trend in vacation policy—so-called "unlimited time off." Companies with this policy don't track employees' time off. Instead, they leave it up to the individual to decide. Call me cynical, but I believe that the impetus of this concept was not to serve employees, but to free businesses of the time and effort to track time off.

More importantly, it allows companies to remove from their financials the accumulated vacation time owed to employees, which appears on the books as a liability and also sometimes requires employers to pay it out upon an employee's departure.

Still looking through that lens of cynicism, the unlimited time off policy appears to provide a lot more benefits to businesses than to employees—businesses no longer have the liability or the requirement to cut checks when employees depart, and employees either don't take the time at all or work while they're away. The business (seemingly!) gets all the benefits and none of the downside.

> **How much time employees report taking off isn't what matters. What matters is whether they actually take the time and whether they work while they are "off."**

I suspect that if you are reading this book, you are not a leader who is interested in exploiting your employees this way. Even if you are viewing the situation from a strictly financial perspective, the "benefits" don't hold up to closer scrutiny. As discussed in the last section, foregoing vacation makes employees less effective in the short term, and isn't a sustainable business strategy in the long term because it leads to burnout and the associated increased costs in absenteeism, health care, and turnover.

Next, let's examine the pros and cons of an unlimited vacation time policy from your employees' perspective. Keep in mind though that it misses the point: how much time employees report taking off isn't what matters. What matters is whether they actually take the time and whether they work while they are "off."

Even at companies without an unlimited vacation time policy, American workers already forfeit a large percentage of their existing paid time off. Research since the pandemic started is still in progress, but early reports suggest that employees are forfeiting one-third to one-half of their vacation time. This suggests that the specific amount of time employees are "allowed" really isn't the issue.

Also, my clients say they work long hours before vacation to prepare for being away and long hours when they get back to catch up. So really, the "vacation time" is more like "work—shifted," with some of the work hours just being subtracted from the days they are gone and added to the days pre- and post-departure.

Lastly, as discussed earlier in the chapter, when workers *do* use their vacation time, they don't *really* disconnect from the office. In my experience, it's almost unheard of that employees don't at least check their email while they are away. My observation aligns with a survey from 2021 that suggested that nearly 90 percent of respondents reported working while on vacation.[viii] And more than half of those—66 percent—said they did so due to a request from their boss. It's true that employees have some responsibility for this: you can only know of work requests if you are checking work communication while you're away.

Your success as a leader depends on the wisdom, experience, and unique perspective that you bring to your work. Your supply of motivation and unique creativity is not endless, and you can't get distance from work if you set aside time during your vacation to check your work messages. You may think you're taking only a short time out of your vacation, but the truth is that reconnecting to work periodically during your time off means that your mind stays engaged in the office, effectively thwarting your opportunity to gain distance, fresh perspective, and a recharge of motivation and creativity.

As someone who wants the best results for your employees and your company's bottom line, you'll want to create an environment that encourages—or requires—total disconnection while away.

How to Evaluate Unlimited Vacation Time

Simply stating that you have an unlimited vacation or PTO policy can initially be helpful in attracting talent but can also create difficulties with existing staff. As with so many things, the advantages and disadvantages are not found in the policy itself but in the implementation. The following is a list of issues to consider before you implement an unlimited time off policy:

Will unlimited PTO complicate your company's ability to adhere to any federal or state laws? Consider, for example, the Family and Medical Leave Act. This requires some employers to offer extended, unpaid, job-protected leave in certain circumstances. Ensure that you understand your company's requirements under this law and how to properly pair it with an unlimited PTO policy. Additionally, some state laws require any unused vacation time to be paid out annually or at termination. This could preclude or complicate an unlimited PTO policy.

Do you currently use extra days off as a reward? How often are they used, and do they produce the intended result? Consider how an unlimited vacation policy will affect using time off as a reward, and what you might offer instead.

How do you feel about the work ethic of your team now? This might give you some insight into whether unlimited PTO might create a problem of employees taking too *much* time or taking too little time.

Do you expect abuse to be a problem? If this concerns you, consider whether the policy will be truly unlimited or whether there will be a ceiling. Also, how will you evaluate abuse? Some leaders tell me they would only be concerned if excessive time off is combined with underperformance. My response in that case is to ask, "On what specific metrics will you evaluate performance? And on what will you base 'high performance' and 'underperformance' classifications?"

Will your tolerance be different based on job role? For example, will leaders' time off be viewed differently than individual contributors' time off?

Do you have managers with outdated performance metrics? It's not uncommon for inexperienced managers to base their evaluation of performance on "face time" at work. This could create an unfair bias against employees who take advantage of the policy, even if they don't abuse it.

How do leaders approach vacation time now? Remember that your culture is created by the behavior of your employees, but no one shapes the culture as much as the leaders. And the higher in the company hierarchy the leader is, the more influence they have on the culture. So whether your leaders take a lot of vacation time or hardly any vacation time, this will impact the behavior of the rest of the team.

Do you have a demanding or otherwise high-pressure culture? A common problem of unlimited time off is not that employees take too much but that they take too little. If your culture is demanding, implementing unlimited PTO is more likely to cause employees to feel guilty about taking the time rather than to be seen as a perk that supports their work-life balance.

Will an unlimited vacation policy cause confusion among the staff? This is common and often leads to underutilization of vacation time. To mitigate this, spell out the policy in detail, in writing, and solicit input from knowledgeable sources, such as peers, members of a business or industry group, an employment attorney, or outsourced or in-house human resources experts. For example, this works only for salaried staff, not hourly staff.

Will you offer any guidelines? And if so, will they support or sabotage the policy? For example, upon implementing an unlimited vacation time policy at Virgin, Richard Branson said, "They are only going to do it when they feel 100 percent comfortable that they and their team are up to date on every project and that their absence will not in any way damage the business—or, for that matter, their careers!"[ix] When is any professional "100 percent comfortable they are up to date on every project?" The very nature of most professional jobs is that there is always more to do than time to do it, and the desire for organizations to run "lean" is prevalent. Also, who will determine whether time off will "damage their career?" This statement from Branson reads more like a warning than a benefit to me.

Will you put in any minimum requirements? If you are concerned that underuse will be a problem (especially if your staff doesn't currently take all their vacation time), you might consider creating minimum requirements and also consecutive days in those minimums. For example, "everyone must take at least five consecutive days at some point in the year." If you implement this, then there is still a tracking burden, but you could just create a shared spreadsheet and instruct all employees to add their time there, which would assist with both tracking and planning. Another alternative to consider is whether there are times of the year that you could just close the company down.

How will this affect your culture? Unlimited PTO is a policy that is based on trust. If you don't currently have a high-trust culture, this policy might just create an additional strain on an already fragile culture.

How will your employees perceive the policy? If you decide to implement an unlimited PTO policy, once you are clear on the details and have them in writing, introduce the policy to your team in advance of it becoming active. Their questions can help inform and improve the policy or at least how the policy is articulated and implemented.

The answers to all these questions require that leadership is in touch with employee sentiment. If you feel that answering these questions would be difficult at your organization, it may be an indication that pulse surveys of employees would be helpful. Consider a tool like 15Five (15Five.com).

Regardless of the type of vacation policy in use at your organization, remember the most important point of this section: how much time employees are offered is less important than whether they actually use the time, and whether they truly disconnect from work while they're gone. *Vacation* is a noun meaning "a period of suspension of work, study, or other activity, usually used for rest, recreation, or travel; recess or holiday" and "freedom or release from duty, business, or activity." Therefore, doing any amount of work while supposedly on vacation means it's not actually a vacation, and the benefits—including increased mental and physical well-being, improved creativity and motivation, renewed inspiration, and resistance to burnout—do not apply.

Learn from Others' Mistakes

If you choose to eliminate your formal vacation policy that requires specifying and tracking the number of days off, it's important to ensure that an unlimited vacation policy doesn't actually turn into no vacation for your employees.

This happened at Netflix, when it was one of the first companies to embrace an unlimited vacation policy. CEO Reed Hastings wrote about this policy in his book *No Rules Rules*, and the years it took the company to get it right.

He offers two pieces of advice, outlined in an article for *Inc.* magazine.[x] His first piece of advice reinforces the influence of leaders that is illustrated throughout this book. He writes, "In the absence of a policy, the amount of vacation people take largely reflects what they see their boss and colleagues taking."

His second piece of advice is that leaders should frequently discuss two things with the team:

1 Appropriate and inappropriate behaviors around vacation

Parameters for the policy, such as how many people in a department can be out at one time and how much advance notice is required

Employee downtime and vacation are important components of company culture, and your company culture deserves thoughtful consideration, especially in light of the postpandemic changes to work. Productivity ultimately suffers when employees skimp on time off or work while they're on vacation. Give your staff the support, policies, and tools they need to truly get away and recharge.

To be more productive and efficient is to make the best use of the resources available to you. In your quest toward productivity, for yourself or your company, don't neglect the most important resources, which are neither time nor money, but body and mind. If your pursuit of productivity or success comes at the expense of you or your team's physical or emotional well-being, it is ultimately destined to fail.

7

How Remote and Hybrid Work Are Changing Business

Remote work has been a part of the business environment for decades, but it was not traditionally favored by business leadership. This was in part because an easy and common metric to determine A players was how much face time they had in the office. Showing up early, staying late, and being at your desk every time someone was looking for you was a sign of dedication to your job. Many leaders want their employees in the office because they believe it promotes engagement, productivity, dedication, teamwork, and innovation. This was a persistent belief because there was very little evidence to the contrary. Even successful businesses with a fully distributed model were viewed as successful in spite of their remote environment, not *because* of it. Because of their limited numbers in the past, successful companies with fully distributed teams could easily be dismissed as outliers.

These leaders now face a reckoning: the remote working that was necessitated due to the coronavirus pandemic proved that face time in the office is not a useful metric on which to evaluate performance. It's also not a useful metric to evaluate engagement. In fact, I think the question before us now is whether it is a useful metric for anything at all. There is now widespread evidence that many businesses—and more importantly, their employees—can not only survive, but thrive, with a fully distributed or hybrid model.

In my experience, many business owners who had all employees in the office before the pandemic want everyone to come back to the office. They tell me, "It just works better," but they have no evidence that supports the assertion. I think a big part of why leaders want everyone back in the office is because it's what they know. It's familiar, and it's comfortable.

For the purposes of discussion, let's simplify success metrics for remote work into just two business success metrics and two individual success metrics:

Business Success Metrics

→ productivity of the employees (more and better outputs with the same amount of inputs)

→ growth of the company (revenue and profits)

Individual Success (Happiness) Metrics

→ the "convenience" offered to employees' personal lives (I will discuss this later in the chapter)

→ accomplishment (employees leave work feeling like they had a productive day versus feeling they were busy all day but got nothing done)

While this list is certainly not exhaustive, it's important. Based on these metrics, the forced work-from-home experiment caused by the pandemic shows that none of these things were harmed and many were improved. (Of course, not all businesses grew their revenue during the pandemic, but enough did to confirm the viability of the model.)

Aside from disruptions caused by the pandemic itself, quite a lot of business occurred during the almost two years of mostly remote work, much the same as it did before.

Defining Remote Work Terms

For the discussion in this chapter, it's useful to be clear about the definition of the various terms used when discussing remote work and the variations of corporate work environments:

→ **Remote work** typically means the same as working from home. However, remote work could also encompass working from somewhere other than the place one lives or is staying (such as a coworking space). One distinction to keep in mind is that remote work typically refers to work done at home or another location *instead of* at the company office. There is also work done at home that is *in addition to* work done at the office.

→ A **distributed** team is one that does not share the same physical work space. This could mean that everyone works in the same city, but from home. Or it could mean that the company has offices around the world, and employees work from these offices. It could also mean that employees work from home without regard to geographic location.

→ **Fully distributed** typically means there is no company office or headquarters. Sometimes organizations with fully distributed teams are referred to as "remote first."

→ **Hybrid** or a hybrid environment means that an organization has one or more offices or headquarters but some or all employees work remotely some or all of the time.

Regardless of what the studies will say about remote work, there is no doubt that it is here to stay. This doesn't mean that every organization will offer it, or that every employee wants it. But remote work has clearly established its place as a staple in the list of benefits an organization does or does not offer.

As the coronavirus recedes from pandemic to endemic, organizations and individuals are struggling—and I expect will continue to struggle for some time—with how to define the "new normal" moving forward, and how to balance the advantages and disadvantages of a fully distributed or hybrid work environment.

Factors to Consider with Remote Work

I often read about factors involved in remote work as being described as binary: good or bad for organizations and people. But the pandemic made clear to me that there is too much nuance to make broad assumptions.

Productivity of work from home is often defined in the

research as hours worked. Increased productivity equals more hours worked, and decreased productivity equals fewer hours worked. But this frame is useless. More hours does not necessarily correlate to more, or better, knowledge work. Furthermore, it's clear that too much work leads to burnout and declining productivity, and it's difficult to isolate that tipping point (although I did offer some research-based guidelines in the last chapter).

The very things that make remote work advantageous to some individuals and companies also make it detrimental, or at least unappealing, to others. In the rest of this section, I'll break out the factors to consider, and how to determine if each of them can be a net positive or a net negative to your specific organization.

Overhead

The primary benefit of remote work to organizations is the same as it's always been: lower overhead in the form of real estate costs, furniture, and equipment. Some companies find it provides an advantage in recruiting, although I expect that advantage to be minimized as working from home continues to normalize and become more widespread.

Organizations are working on ways to get the benefits of lower real estate costs while also luring employees back to the office. Personal offices have mostly been eliminated except for those dedicated to the most senior staff. Everyone else gets open spaces, "cubicle farms," or "hot desks," all of which I will discuss in a later chapter. The personal work space is no longer being used as an enticement to overcome the preference to work from home. Instead it's the other perks, like free chef-prepared meals, dry-cleaning services, and on-site games and fitness centers. Although the one benefit that would likely make the biggest difference in luring people back to the office is on-site childcare,[i] as of this writing, I couldn't find any research-based or even anecdotal evidence that this is on the rise.

Productivity and Hours Worked

Most research shows that employees work more hours when working from home. Often the conclusion drawn is that employees are therefore more productive, but this isn't necessarily true.

Knowledge work—regardless of the location of the work—requires measurement beyond time observed at one's desk and even time spent on a computer. I have made the argument at various points in this book that the most important job of a knowledge worker is thinking. Certainly some of that is thinking about a task a worker is doing on a computer, but important thinking time also happens away from the computer and from a desk.

The rise of remote work provides incentives to find more objective and results-based performance measurements, which benefits the organization in the long run. I believe that if other useful metrics for evaluating knowledge work were available, it would be easier for organizations to embrace remote work. In the last chapter, I'll discuss my recommendation for a more useful productivity metric.

Trust

Another factor that is creating an obstacle to the widespread corporate adoption of remote work is trust, which is more complicated than it may seem.

It's difficult to get to know people, and therefore to trust them, when you are never in the same physical location. Often, we begin building trust with someone by shaking hands when we first meet. This touch, and other casual interactions that occur when we meet face-to-face in professional situations, prime the brain to release chemicals associated with trust and empathy.[ii] As a result, people who see each other in person frequently can find it easier to form trusting relationships.

Employers must trust that their employees are being responsible and accountable. But here again, these terms are subject to interpretation and are difficult to identify. The way a leader will define "responsible and accountable" will be different for each leader and each organization. Here are some questions to ask to arrive at the right conclusions for you, your team, and your organization:

→ **What** specifically do you need to trust your employees to do?

→ **When** do you need to trust them to do it?

→ **How** will you evaluate whether you can trust them?

When I ask leaders what they need to trust their employees to do, often the answer I receive is, "I need to trust that they are working." But this isn't specific enough. When I probe they tell me they need to trust that employees are "getting their jobs done," "pulling their weight," and "making customers happy." But all of these terms are subject to a wide range of interpretation. Have a discussion with each of your team members about what behaviors and outcomes from them will earn your trust. Following are questions that provide criteria you can use to evaluate trustworthiness in your team that are more specific and less prone to misunderstanding:

→ They are keeping their commitments.

→ They are meeting their deadlines.

→ They are producing work that is accurate and meets or exceeds the quality standards of your organization.

→ Their customers are happy with their work outputs.

> **If your team members earn your trust through the behaviors you identify, do you care exactly how many hours they work or when specifically they work those hours?**

Another answer I receive from leaders when I ask them about the trust they place in their employees is, "I need them to be accessible." This is another word that is widely subjective. Accessible when? If you're thinking "during the workday" or "if there is an emergency," that's a reasonable answer, but only if you have specifically defined *workday* and *emergency*. Also, how will they find out you have an emergency? If you communicate emergencies through email, for example, then they still have to be checking their email all the time, watching for emergencies.

One poor result of basing trust on accessibility is that employees try to make up for their lack of physical presence in the office by working longer hours and being always available via email. This reinforces the "always on" culture and other factors that lead to burnout.

Other questions you should examine for yourself: if your team members earn your trust through the behaviors you identify, do you care exactly how many hours they work or when specifically they work those hours? These are important questions to answer and convey to your employees, regardless of whether they typically work in the same physical space as you.

Answering the questions posed in this section will put you on the path to identifying the metrics of productivity that are useful and relevant to you, your department, and your organization.

Talent Pool

When the pool of talent is unconstrained by geographic location and physical limitations, it can expand the diversity of voices in an organization.

Prior to the coronavirus pandemic, many organizations resisted language in the Americans with Disabilities Act and discounted the idea that remote work was a "reasonable accommodation" and that it could still allow employees to do "essential job duties." The pandemic has removed the basis for that resistance.

Companies that embrace remote work can open employment opportunities to those who have a hard time in an office environment. It's hard to understate the variety of day-to-day details that can pose a challenge to people who have visible and invisible disabilities and sensitivities. Everything from physical inaccessibility to excessive sensory input can create an obstacle to successful employment.

Companies with a central location where employees report to an office tend to draw their talent pool from the local area. In some cases, this can result in a similarity of backgrounds and ethnicities. Remote work typically makes it easier to have an inclusive workforce that is represented by a wide diversity of people from a variety of backgrounds and ethnicities.

Remove work can expand the pool of qualified applicants. This will be increasingly important as the job market and the race for talent continue to become more and more competitive.

Team Collaboration

Working remotely can make people feel disconnected and isolated, especially when they're geographically distant and rarely, if ever, see their coworkers in person. In-person time fosters community and reminds employees that they are involved in something bigger than themselves.

Add a line item to the budget for annual (or more frequent, if possible) team get-togethers. If there are staff who are within a few hours' drive of each other, encourage them to get together more often by renting coworking space where they can meet or simply work side-by-side periodically.

8

Necessary Commitments for Successful Hybrid and Remote Teams

Work-life boundaries and effective communication are issues that affect most organizations. But since the start of the pandemic, companies have doubled down: they are making a rock-solid commitment to both asynchronous communication and a healthy work-life balance.

Moving to mostly asynchronous communication represents quite a shift from the instant gratification you can get by working with team members in the same physical space. And work-life balance is always important, of course, but now that work space and personal space have become the same thing, the commitment becomes exponentially more important.

Just saying the words doesn't cut it. Leaders need to demonstrate the company's commitments and take corrective action when team members stray. Otherwise, the entire foundation for a high-functioning remote culture begins to erode.

Before we further discuss the commitments to asynchronous communication and healthy work-life balance for teams moving to fully or partially distributed, we need to discuss why they are important. So let's take a closer look at the idea first addressed in the introduction: the raw material for knowledge work is thinking, and optimal "thinking work" depends on the physical and emotional well-being of the thinker (the employee).

A culture that has an emphasis on synchronous (real-time) communication tends to be higher-pressure, more stressful, and promotes unhealthy work habits. Asynchronous communication is slower, but it's also more thoughtful and less stressful.

Leaders Can't Control Well-Being, But They Can Influence It

Optimal knowledge work is the product of brain function. Therefore, it is dependent on how your brain is functioning at any given moment. And there are two components of brain function: the physical functioning of the tangible organ, and the general emotional state of the person.

Physical State

The functioning of the brain depends on your physical well-being—sleep, hydration, exercise—in a given moment. The brain uses more energy than any other organ in the body, so glucose levels are also important (which depend on eating habits). All these factors influence how the brain is functioning as an organ.

Given the fact that the brain is a knowledge worker's most important tool, you should care about how your team members' brains are functioning during work hours. This is the same logic that concludes that if you managed a team of carpenters, it would matter to you if your team went to work every day with dull saws, or if you managed a team of drivers and their cars didn't have properly working brakes.

As you read this, you might be thinking that it's much easier to ensure saws and cars are operating properly than brains. Physical well-being is controlled by the individual, so you may conclude that you have no control over your team members' physical well-being. You'd be correct for thinking that, but while it's true that you can't control these issues, you can *influence* them.

Ups and downs in our energy levels happen naturally throughout the day. These peaks and valleys are affected by overall wellness but also by our physical state in a given moment. And this is where leaders have influence. When we hit an energy lull during our days, most of us reach for sugar, caffeine, maybe nicotine, but none of these provide a sustainable energy boost, and all of them have a "rebound" effect that has the potential to leave us with less energy than before.

There are two things that provide the easiest and most sustainable energy boost—sleep and physical activity—both of which leaders can influence, at least during the workday (although it's admittedly more challenging to influence remote employees).

Sleep

The Centers for Disease Control calls sleep deprivation in the United States a public health epidemic.[i] This is because most adults get an average of four to six hours of sleep per night, but the human body functions best on seven to nine hours of sleep per night. Of course, we can function on fewer than seven hours of sleep per night, but most of us can't perform optimally, and the effects are cumulative. When less than seven hours becomes the norm, brain function declines over time.[ii] The increase in degenerative brain diseases that we have seen over the last few decades—like Alzheimer's and dementia—are now known to be related to too little sleep.

The point about sleep is that one of the best things we can do to provide sustainable energy and increase our brain function in a given moment is take a short catnap—anywhere from five to twenty minutes. Staying asleep for more than twenty minutes risks entering REM sleep, and awakening from REM sleep causes the groggy, sleep hangover feeling that is not conducive to peak performance during the workday. But studies show that a short nap is refreshing and offers a powerful and sustainable energy boost. And the best news for people who think they couldn't nap at work? Research indicates that just resting provides almost the same benefits, even if sleep isn't achieved.

You can't control how much sleep your employees get every evening, but you can influence their brain functioning by encouraging napping during the workday, whether employees are in the office or at home. If you have the authority to create one or more quiet spaces for your team members to use in the office, that's a useful step. If you don't, look for other ways to encourage employees to have some quiet time during their workday. Maybe even encourage them to go sit in their cars for a break if necessary. There is a "rest continuum," where actual sleep during a nap time is the best, but if not sleep, then resting with eyes closed is the next best thing, and if there isn't anywhere to do that safely, then just some quiet time away from screens, such as sitting outside or even in a break room with no electronic devices, can be helpful. As a leader, you can both model this behavior and encourage employees to follow suit.

Physical Activity

The second factor that offers a fast and easy way to change our energy levels and improve our brain performance during the workday is physical activity. When we move our bodies, it makes our hearts pump more, providing more oxygen to our blood cells. When that oxygenated blood reaches our brains, it improves cognitive performance in both the short term and the long term.

Over the last few decades, things like foosball tables, Ping-Pong, and indoor basketball hoops have become more prevalent office fixtures. The most obvious reason is to create a work environment that is more fun. But an even more important reason is because taking a break to engage in a few minutes of physical activity will allow you to perform better after the break than if a break consisted of remaining at your desk and reading news or social media. A full-blown workout is not required to get the benefits (although I fully support on-site fitness centers). Any sort of activity—like a walk, a trip up and down a flight of stairs, or an on-site physical game—is very likely to improve mental alertness and acuity. Consider taking outdoor walks during your days in the office and inviting team members to join you.

Again, leaders can't control whether employees get sufficient exercise on a regular basis, but they can certainly influence whether team members move their bodies while in the office. If your team is remote, consider doing some calls by phone and encouraging participants to walk around their neighborhood while talking. Simply asking employees when you connect with them if they have taken any breaks or stood up from their desks can be all the encouragement they need to improve their brain function during the workday.

Emotional State

The second component that affects brain output is emotional state—mood, feelings, and stress levels. If a person is cranky, overwhelmed, and stressed, that's going to have a detrimental impact on their cognition and decision-making.[iii]

You likely hired your knowledge worker team members—at least in part—for their attitude, their outlook, and their "culture fit," which includes things like their work ethic and their ability to get along with others. It's difficult to have a positive attitude and to get along well with others when we are feeling stressed and overwhelmed. It makes us feel cranky and impacts our capacity to do high-quality knowledge work, because it interferes with our ability to think clearly, communicate productively, collaborate, and cooperate.

When I ask audiences what makes a good day at work, typically the first answer I receive is "Getting stuff done!" When we accomplish more of our important work, we feel satisfied and content at the end of our workdays, sometimes even inspired and energized. In contrast, when we're distracted and busy all day—jumping from task to task, having rapid-fire conversations on different topics, and attending meeting after meeting with no breaks in between—we feel like we don't accomplish anything of value. It's demotivating, stressful, and exhausting.

We feel good about our jobs and enjoy them more when we have days that end with a feeling of accomplishment. I think it's fair to say that everyone prefers to have days (with the exception of some vacation days) that we can reflect back on and think, "Wow, I got so much done!" instead of days when we think, "I was busy all day and yet I got nothing done!"

Research conducted at Harvard on creative work inside organizations led to the discovery that "ordinary scientists, marketers, programmers, and other unsung knowledge workers, whose jobs require creative productivity every day, have more in common with famous innovators than most managers realize. The workday events that ignite their emotions, fuel their motivation, and trigger their perceptions are fundamentally the same." Their studies led these researchers to coin "the progress principle," which states, "Of all the things that can boost emotions, motivation, and perceptions during a workday, the single most important is making progress in meaningful work. And the more frequently people experience that sense of progress, the more likely they are to be creatively productive in the long run."[iv]

The takeaway for leaders of knowledge workers is that if you want to motivate your team members and help them be "creatively productive," you need to help them get more of their important work done on a daily basis. Leaders like you need to look for things that are interfering with your team's ability to get important work done. Not only is this good for employees, it's of course an important contributor to organizational success.

Productivity must be evaluated and improved on two levels: the individual level and the organizational level, because the productivity of individuals doesn't exist in a vacuum. The context is important. Organizational culture and leadership behavior can unintentionally interfere with team members' ability to get their important work done.

Now that we know about the importance of brain function in optimizing knowledge work, let's turn back to how committing to asynchronous communication and work-life balance can improve the productivity of knowledge workers as you fully embrace remote or hybrid work.

9

The Problem with Synchronous Communication and Remote Work

Remember the days when someone would pass by your desk and you'd say, "Hey, do you have a minute?" Or at the end of a meeting, someone might say, "Hey, can you answer a quick question?" Back then, we communicated in real time with our colleagues, and it was often fast and efficient.

Then came the pandemic.

Most knowledge workers went remote. We were no longer in the same physical space as our colleagues, but many of us continued using the same synchronous, real-time communication style. The only difference now is that rather than catching someone walking by your desk, you send an instant message or a text whenever you have a thought to share or a question to ask.

However, there's a big problem with that.

Attempting to rely mainly on synchronous communications in the digital space is neither efficient nor effective. Synchronous communication happens in real time, with immediate responses. A Zoom conversation and a phone call, for example, are synchronous.

When we worked in offices, we interacted physically with a limited number of people in a given day, but now that we're working remotely, it feels like everyone is suddenly within our reach. You might have fifty or one hundred colleagues and clients contacting you via instant message, text, or email in a single day. They just want to share a quick thought or ask a quick question. And you likely feel pressure not only to respond, but also to respond immediately.

In the new remote work or hybrid work environment, leaders need to help their teams rethink how they communicate. We can no longer communicate intuitively; to improve our focus and our productivity, we must make a conscious shift to rely more on asynchronous communication.

Asynchronous communication is slower but more thoughtful. Unlike synchronous communication, asynchronous communication doesn't happen in real time and doesn't require an immediate response.

Help your team members shift to using more asynchronous communication. In doing so, you'll enable them to stave off burnout and unleash their genius in the service of your team's most important goals.

Asynchronous Communication Tools

There are a variety of tools you can use to communicate asynchronously with clients or colleagues. You can record a message on Zoom or on a voice recorder on your phone and then attach the recording to an email. You can create a screencast using a tool like QuickTime Player that comes native on Macs. A screencast is a video of what's happening on a computer screen, with a voice-over narration.

Team communication tools drive many of us batty, since we get a drip of half-baked ideas and half-baked requests all day long. And one conversation is constantly interrupted by another.

While most people use Slack and Teams chat as synchronous communication tools, it's much more productive for a company to set a policy of using them as asynchronous tools. This way, anyone on the platform will know they are not expected to respond to every message immediately. (If necessary, designate a few select channels to remain synchronous.) This is why I recommend Twist (twistapp.com) to my clients for team communication. Since it's built on the premise of asynchronous communication, team members can be more thoughtful and less distracted while working.

When Asynchronous Communication Is Better

There are many good uses for asynchronous communication, including company updates, team updates, or project updates.

You could also email a screencast of your presentation with a note that says, "If you have any questions, please email me. I'll answer them at my earliest convenience." This allows you to provide more thoughtful feedback than answering queries on the fly, as you'd need to do with live questions during a presentation.

Asynchronous communication can also work better for collecting feedback or assigning tasks to others.

Synchronous Communication Tools

Even with remote work, there are definitely times when synchronous communication is the most effective strategy. In fact, synchronous communication is invaluable when used for the right purpose.

Tools for synchronous communication include in-person meetings, Zoom meetings, and phone calls. (If you have synchronous online meetings, it can sometimes be helpful to record these and share them asynchronously. This way, anyone present can review the content later, or anyone who couldn't attend can get up to speed.)

Many people use texting as a synchronous communication tool, but this is a mistake. If you text someone an important work-related task, your message is easily buried by the most recent text the recipient receives. Further, when someone is reading your message on the go, it can be hard for them to turn your request into a to-do on their task list.

Instead, use texts for immediate, synchronous communication that often doesn't require a response, such as "I'm running five minutes late. Please start the meeting without me."

As previously discussed, many leaders view email as a synchronous communication tool and expect instant replies to their messages. This sabotages your direct reports' and others' ability to focus on their most important work.

When Synchronous Communication Is Better

Synchronous communication is better for socializing, complex or sensitive discussions when you want to monitor responses and protect feelings, and one-on-one meetings between managers and direct reports. Also, it's better to plan synchronous communication, so rather than sending a (synchronous) instant message that reads "Can you talk?" send an (asynchronous) email that reads "I have a few things I'd like to discuss with you. Can you get on Zoom with me for ten minutes at 3:00 p.m. or 4:00 p.m.?"

Of course, if there's a matter that is truly urgent or time sensitive, then synchronous communication is necessary, but it's helpful to give employees guidance about which tools to use in which situations.

First, you need to decide for your team which tools are generally for synchronous communication and which are generally for asynchronous communication. Then you need to identify when to use each tool and for what purpose. You may need a different version of this chart for clients.

COMMUNICATION GUIDELINES (SAMPLE)

Types of Communication	During Work Hours	Outside Work Hours
Email (asynchronous)	Routine requests, information sharing	Hold or use delay send
Team communication tools (Slack, Teams, Twist, etc.) (asynchronous)	Project-related communication, socializing	Everyone set to Do Not Disturb
Phone, video calls (synchronous)	Relationship-building, sensitive or complex topics (scheduled in advance when possible)	Time-sensitive or urgent only
Text (synchronous)	Time-sensitive or urgent only	Time-sensitive or urgent only

A WORD ABOUT BRAINSTORMING

· ·

Contrary to popular opinion, brainstorming should not be a solely synchronous activity. In fact, the most effective way to brainstorm is through a combination of asynchronous and synchronous communication. Here's how to get the best results:

- Ask people to prepare for the brain-storming session asynchronously and send three ideas to the meeting organizer in advance.
- Plan a meeting to collaborate syn-chronously, whether over Zoom or in person. During the meeting, group similar ideas together.
- Next, engage in a free-flowing dis-cussion to evaluate the pros and cons of each set of ideas.

Working through a brainstorm in this way allows all participants to be more thoughtful than

> brainstorming on the fly without any forethought.
> It also avoids groupthink. Using this technique to
> brainstorm is likely to yield the widest diversity
> of thought and the most creative insights.

Video Meeting Fatigue

Video meeting fatigue is a challenge of remote work, but if you get intentional, there are ways that you can help your team take full advantage of this great technology that has made remote work possible without letting it become a drain on your happiness or your productivity.

It's often known as "Zoom fatigue" or "Zoom gloom," but to be fair, it's the exhaustion caused by days packed with video meetings, regardless of the platform. It happens not only on Zoom but on Microsoft Teams, GoToMeeting, Webex, Google Meet, and all other video platforms. Here are several suggestions for taking the tedium out of video calls.

Don't let meetings crowd out other work. In my experience with clients, I'm hearing that people are on video calls all day. Full days of meetings aren't realistic, so employing the asynchronous communication strategies discussed in the prior section will result in fewer meetings and free up time to get important work done.

Block time between meetings. When all meetings run for thirty minutes or sixty minutes (or end late), this results in back-to-back meetings for long stretches, which is detrimental to high-quality knowledge work for several reasons. First, there's no opportunity for you to process your thoughts and action items from the last meeting before you jump into the next meeting. So meetings become less productive because you don't have a chance to capture action items, and often don't complete them. Second, you don't have an opportunity to make a mindful shift—to consciously bring the last topic to a close and mentally gather your thoughts for the next topic. Lastly, you don't have an opportunity to attend to personal needs, like movement, restroom breaks, water, coffee, or snacks. These last two reasons may prevent you from being present and offering your best insights, so meetings aren't as productive as they could be.

Not every call has to be video. The widespread adoption of video calls has seemed to create an assumption that all calls will now be on video. While face-to-face conversations can be helpful, every call you take doesn't need to be on video. Audio-only calls can free people from their desks and give them an opportunity to take a walk or just move around their space during a meeting, and as discussed earlier, physical movement stimulates cognitive activity.

> **Don't assume all team members know how to use the relevant features of your video meeting platform.**

Don't assume proficiency with the platform. You may expect that "everyone knows this by now." As a professional speaker and trainer who hosts many virtual meetings weekly, I can tell you that not everyone knows many of the following features. Frequent updates to applications also cause us all to have to relearn things we thought we knew. So provide specific instruction, especially on those features that contribute to video meeting exhaustion, such as the following:

→ How to use speaker view, gallery view, and pin video. Without a complete understanding of these features, calls can feel a little frantic when the window "jumps" to a new image every time someone coughs or shuffles a paper.

→ How to hide self view. Watching ourselves on camera contributes to fatigue because it's hard not to be conscious of how we look or how we're behaving. (Although it does remind us that others can see us!)

→ How to use feedback features such as the applause and raise hand icons. Seeing someone else use these but not knowing how can be distracting and cause people to multitask—trying to pay attention to what's being said while also trying to figure out how things work.

→ The difference between meeting and webinar functions. In most platforms, meetings allow everyone to be on camera and are more collaborative. Webinars have only one person on camera, and all the interaction happens via chat. During a virtual event, people may be unclear whether they are visible to the speaker and others. So clarify this at the beginning.

Choose the best view for your meeting type. Once everyone understands the various view and platform features, encourage the team to try them out in real meetings to find what settings increase engagement and reduce fatigue. Consider gallery view for small collaborative meetings where all participants can keep cameras and microphones on. For meetings that are collaborative but one person is expected to do most of the talking, consider having everyone pin the video of the speaker. For meetings with presentations, try speaker view with cameras on but all other microphones (besides the presenter) muted.

VIDEO MEETING SUGGESTED SETTINGS

Meeting Type	View Settings	Cameras	Microphones
Small, collaborative	Gallery	On	On
Larger, collaborative, one primary speaker	Speaker view	On	Muted except when speaking
Presentations	Pin speaker, minimize others	On	Muted except when speaking

Set meeting expectations at the start. Because you're taking a meeting on your computer, it's hard to resist the temptation of having email and other work visible, and even reading it during meeting time. At the beginning of your meetings, explicitly request that participants close any open windows on their screens other than the meeting window. Say something like "I'd like us all to be present for this meeting. Please close your email, close your chat, put your phone on silent, and expand the meeting window to full screen. This will make our meeting run much more efficiently." Also, if participants are permitted to keep their cameras off, it's easier for them to "check out." There are times when this is appropriate, but if you're having a video call, encourage camera use. If you don't feel that seeing other meeting participants is necessary, regular phone calls or conference calls without video are still an option.

Minimize the distraction of virtual backgrounds. Many people don't want to have to clean up their homes, or they share their living space with others, which is a great reason to use these backgrounds. If people are going to use them, don't let the background become a distraction. Encourage the team to share some undistracting image or to use the plainer options that come standard. Some platforms allow you to simply blur your surroundings rather than adding a background image, which is a good option.

Consider disabling all chat in meetings, and private chat in webinars. Text that pops up on the screen while others are speaking is supremely distracting, and private, side conversations are also disrespectful to the speaker and the others in the meeting. Chat encourages your meeting attendees to multitask, and prevents full presence in the meeting.

Begin meetings with a connecting activity. Forging connections between team members or across organizations is absolutely critical for remote workers. This can't be an afterthought or an optional activity when your team is remote. Opportunities for interacting need to be intentionally included in every meeting and not just relegated to HR-sponsored virtual coffee chats. My friend, remote work author, and leadership expert Kevin Eikenberry offers the following advice to his clients: whenever possible, try to start your meetings with a short connection activity, maybe four to six minutes. Put each pair of workers into a breakout room to discuss a fun, non-work-related question. Each person answers for two minutes, and then the partners switch. Or start with an icebreaker question such as, "Share one word that best describes how you're feeling right now." **Don't overthink these exercises or try to get too fancy.** Just remember that work topics should be off-limits because you want to build connections and relationships. Do these exercises at the beginning of the meeting. Putting the connecting activity first signals the importance of fostering interaction and sets a great tone for the rest of the session.

Lead Your Team to Make the Shift

You can help your remote workers thrive by leaning into asynchronous work. This means limiting the number of video-based meetings to only those whose goals can't be achieved in other ways. As a leader, you need to spare employees from days full of endless video meetings. Then take steps to ensure the meetings you do hold help workers connect with each other in addition to achieving other project-related goals.

Do you always try to be available in real time to all your colleagues and clients? In attempting (uselessly!) to run faster and work harder to achieve this goal, you're at risk of burning out.

Instead, work consciously to shift to using more asynchronous communication. You'll relieve the building pressure on yourself and your team, and you'll all be able to work less frantically and more thoughtfully.

10

Work-Life Balance

Work-life balance is a solution to the negative impacts of work, including high pressure, stress, and burnout. But work-life balance has been a topic of intense discussion for decades, and the problem of workplace pressure, stress, and burnout continues to grow.

This is because we are not defining work-life balance properly.

Society offers several definitions of work-life balance. Some employees are more likely to say that their work-life balance improves when they can work from home. But my experience suggests that those who say this are defining work-life balance as "making it easier and more convenient to manage my personal life."

I wholeheartedly agree that it's helpful and convenient and makes our lives easier when we can manage our personal lives without interference from work. In addition, it enables us to take less time off and prevents exposure to airborne illnesses, reducing sick time and health-care costs. Also, working from home offers some of us (but not all!) solitude and seclusion that we may view as a big advantage over working in an open area or cubicle with its corresponding loss of privacy.

When our workplace is our home, we can walk the dog, work out, run a quick errand, throw in a load of laundry, prep dinner, go to a doctor's appointment, and care for a sick family member all while still doing varying amounts of work *and* while mostly keeping these behaviors hidden from others.

When we must report to an office for work, some of these are impossible, and the rest require us to receive permission from, provide an explanation to, or balance the expectations of other people. This freedom from permission/explanation/ expectations is what makes working from home easier and more convenient. It allows us to fill small gaps in our workday with personal tasks and activities, so we can get more of those done. We might say that working from home allows us to be productive in our personal lives while working, and this is why many people like it—especially primary caregivers in a household.

I also hear some people—especially those who love their jobs—bristle at the term *work-life balance*. These people tend to define work-life balance as the requirement that we give the same amount of time to "working" vs. "not working." This equal time doesn't sit well with those who love their jobs, because they *want* to work. They enjoy their work. Their work inspires them in ways that other parts of their lives don't.

The combination of the freedom definition I described earlier and the equal time requirement definition is probably why the term *work-life integration* was coined and why it is often seen as a more appealing alternative to *work-life balance*. It more adequately describes the freedom I described and perhaps sounds more appealing to those who work long hours because they love their work so much.

However, when I think of "work-life integration," I'm more likely to imagine parents checking their email from the soccer field than I am to imagine the situation I described earlier. Work-life integration sounds more to me like work intruding into our personal time than the other way around.

I'm convinced that the term *work-life balance* is the appropriate term, because it sounds closer to what we are trying to achieve as individuals and as a society. However, I would humbly like to propose a new definition of work-life balance that enables it to truly provide a solution to negative by-products of work like pressure, stress, and burnout.

Defining Work-Life Balance for Your Team

It's never been more urgent for leaders to define work-life balance expectations for their workforce. It's true that you can't *give* your employees work-life balance. They have to decide for themselves whether they will take it. But a major consideration in their decision is how their work-life balance will affect their careers and how they are perceived in the organization. And that means that leaders have a lot of influence over the decisions that employees make.

So I have a specific definition of the term *work-life balance* that I believe will be helpful for leaders to adopt, share with their employees, and use in making decisions about remote and hybrid work environments.

My definition is simple: don't work too much. No matter how much someone loves their work or how demanding they feel it is, there is ample research showing that (especially) knowledge workers perform optimally and stave off burnout when they also do other things. As discussed in detail in prior sections, limiting your work hours will help you recharge your creativity and get a fresh perspective, both necessary for high-quality knowledge work.

Wondering what's "too much"? A variety of studies show that working more than forty-five hours per week is detrimental to both physical and mental health.[i] A 2014 study by John Pencavel of Stanford showed that productivity per hour declines around fifty hours per week, and working more than fifty-five hours is pointless.[ii] And a study by time management author Laura Vanderkam showed that around thirty-eight hours of work per week produces the happiest employees.[iii]

When we do something often, we strengthen the neural pathways in our brains that are related to this activity. This is why practicing a skill makes us better at that skill. But knowledge work is less a skill than it is a way that we uniquely combine inputs—ideas, analysis, knowledge, data—into unique and coherent outputs. The more diverse the inputs, the more creative and unique the outputs. The more we do *other things* in addition to work—movies, television, books, travel, conversation, new sights, tastes, smells, experiences—the more new neural pathways we can create, and this is an important way of increasing creativity. Additionally, when our focus is narrow, creative changes are more likely to be incremental, based on what is already known—more like refining existing ideas. But divergent thinking based on a greater diversity of inputs causes more transformative thinking. So it's important to realize that sometimes the best thing we can do for our work is not work!

In our digital age, it's all too easy to message employees outside business hours or even when they're on vacation. And employees feel increasing pressure to respond to messages from the dinner table, the kids' soccer game—even from bed in the middle of the night!

During the pandemic, I lost count of the times I heard someone say, *"I'm not taking any time off from work because there is nothing else to do."* I understand that they were probably referring to things that were restricted by the pandemic, like dining out, travel, moviegoing, concerts, etc. But I also couldn't help but wonder at their dismissal of the vast number of things that were still available to us, even during the pandemic—things like reading, exercise, outdoor activities, cooking, and a practically unlimited number of hobbies and learning opportunities.

So let your team know that you define work-life balance simply as "not working too much," because this allows them to focus on three components critical to optimal knowledge work: physical well-being, emotional well-being, and creativity. This definition overcomes the failings of the freedom definition, because it makes clear that the location of work is not the primary problem. It also overcomes the failings of the equal time definition, because the level of enjoyment one gets from work is also not the issue.

Work with your team to set expectations around how many hours they work per week, knowing research suggests that somewhere between 38 and 45 hours is optimal. Work-life balance, when defined this way, not only can be the solution to the negative consequences of work (pressure, stress, burnout), but can also provide the key to unlocking your team members' creativity and innovation that will give your business an edge.

And remember that leaders are part of the team, so everything here is true for you as well. The expectations you set as a team won't take hold if you and other leaders don't practice what you preach.

Flextime Becomes Always On

Prior to the pandemic, when more people worked in the same physical space, most everyone showed up and left around the same time, give or take an hour or two. This was commonly referred to as "business hours," and if someone wanted to deviate from those hours, they asked to work on a different schedule. For example, prior to the pandemic, most office staff worked in the office from 8 a.m. or 9 a.m. to 5 p.m. or 6 p.m., give or take. If someone wanted to work, say, 11 a.m. to

7 p.m., typically they would ask for permission. If permission was granted, this was a form of "flextime."

But when the pandemic forced us to work remotely, everyone's hours reverted to what was most convenient for them based on the needs of their family, and permission was not sought or expected.

Remote work naturally leads to flextime. When people don't work in an office, traditional "office hours" erode. Employees with small children might be getting the majority of their work done at night after the kids are in bed. Others are working early and hoping to quit early. Still others are starting late and working late.

So without a demonstrated commitment to the team's work-life balance, the flextime offered by remote work quickly turns into "always on," which erodes the boundaries around personal time and leads to burnout.

If everyone on your team is working different hours, you may be getting emails and messages at all hours of the day, night, or weekend—which can quickly create an always available or "always on" environment.

Once an always on expectation takes root in your company culture, it becomes difficult, if not impossible, to reset later. While many businesses have around-the-clock operations, it still doesn't mean that all employees can be working around the clock. Always on isn't sustainable at the individual level. It increases pressure, quickly turns your company into an unpleasant place to work, and might cause even the most dedicated employees to consider other offers. Here are some ways to prevent remote working and flextime from becoming always on.

Address the problem head-on. Explicitly acknowledge the problem, and emphasize the importance of downtime. This can be done in a virtual town hall, which is a useful practice to keep everyone connected if your team is remote. These town halls can be live or recorded messages from the CEO and senior leadership. I recommend executing these leadership communications on a regular basis and repeating the importance of downtime frequently for reinforcement. The message can be something like this: "We believe that downtime is important, and we recommend that you track the hours you spend working, and limit those to roughly forty hours a week. Depending on your role, there may be times when more hours are required, but we expect and encourage you to balance busier times with intermittently lighter schedules." It may be tempting to refrain from giving this implicit instruction, especially during times when outside factors (pandemic, inflation, civil unrest, etc.) are putting pressure on your organization, but a large body of research shows it will have a positive impact on your culture in the long term.

Provide guidelines for communication channels. First, establish clear guidelines about which communication channel should be used in which situation. (The communication guidelines chart earlier in this chapter should be helpful.) Then define clear communication hours (for example, 8:00 a.m. to 6:00 p.m.). Outside those hours, employees should be encouraged to change their settings to "Do Not Disturb" and to use the schedule send feature of their email client so that messages only get delivered during communication hours. You can use a version of this even if your company spans multiple time zones.

If any correspondence must happen outside the set communication hours, such as for urgent or time-sensitive issues, make them phone or text only. This way, people can comfortably close down all other communication channels like email, Slack, instant messenger, etc. The act of having to call or text someone is usually enough to give the sender a pause to think, "Do I really need this person now, or can the communication wait?" This allows everyone on your team to work whenever is appropriate for them but not feel like they have to work all the time to accommodate everyone else's schedule.

Use technology to your advantage. Consider technology solutions to help reinforce the behavior, such as programming the corporate server so even if emails are sent outside communication hours, they aren't delivered until the designated times. Check if your team collaboration tools have global settings so everyone is automatically set to "Do Not Disturb" mode outside the designated communication hours.

Model the desired behavior. Finally, remember the influence leaders have, not only on employees but also on their families and communities. Leaders must model the behavior, or else it will never work. If you create communication guidelines in your organization, then anyone in the organization who manages others should work hard to follow the guidelines themselves and also reward and discourage behaviors accordingly. For example, saying, "thanks for being so responsive" to someone who answers an email outside the defined communication hours sends a mixed message and will undermine the guidelines and, ultimately, trust.

After-Hours Emails Are Worse Than You Think

The pandemic blurred the boundary between work and personal life. A study conducted during the pandemic found that 70 percent of remote workers were clocking time on the weekends.[iv]

This meant that even more work emails were flying in and out of inboxes 24/7, and many professionals couldn't resist the urge to check them, even when waking up for a quick minute in the middle of the night. No one wants to work too much, but it's especially hard to avoid messages when we think those messages might be from our boss. So if you are a leader, don't underestimate the influence you have on your team members! It doesn't matter what you say; it's what you do that matters.

Sending just one after-hours work email can cause a cascade of negative effects for you, the recipient of your message, and even the recipient's family!

Studies reveal that employees experience increased anxiety, decreased quality of sleep, and lower relationship satisfaction because after-hours emails promote the constant feeling that a message from work could arrive at any moment, regardless of the time of day or day of the week. One researcher, Bill Becker from Virginia Tech, called this "anticipatory stress"—the feeling of always being ready to receive a work email after hours, even if one never arrives.

Surprisingly, his study found that it wasn't just the employee who experienced negative health effects from never being able to disconnect from work; the partners of employees also experienced the same negative outcomes.

So before you hit "send" on what seems to you to be just one quick question while it's on your mind, ask yourself if sending that question now is more important than supporting your colleague's quality of life.

And yes, your team members have responsibility and control over whether they check emails. In fact, my message to busy team members is that if you're checking your work email on nights and weekends, work isn't "invading" your personal life—you're inviting it in! But as a leader, consider that it's absolutely easier not to check work emails when you know your boss isn't sending them.

You may hear team members say something like, "Yes, I don't really work on the weekend. I just answer a few emails." Here's the mistake in that thinking: email is work! And it keeps employees' minds engaged in their professional responsibilities, preventing them from getting some relaxation. And even if you don't care about their relaxation, managing emails on the weekend prevents them from getting distance from their work and the fresh perspective that comes with it.

The strategies in this book for communication guidelines, communication hours, downtime, and other policies—coupled with consistent implementation of these policies by leaders—can help employees draw a clear line between their work and personal lives. By refraining from sending emails after hours, you'll help your team truly unplug, reduce their anticipatory stress, and possibly even increase the quality of their sleep and their relationships.

Remember, leaders are knowledge workers too, so

everything that is true for your team members is also true for you. It's best for you to stay off your email during your downtime, but if you must compose messages outside work hours, schedule them to be sent at an appropriate time to spare your team from the negative consequences of after-hours emails.

Although the steps vary, most email programs and services include options for scheduling messages to be sent at a later time.

→ Microsoft Outlook: Select Delay Delivery in the Options tab of the message. Or try Mailbird, a full-featured alternative to Outlook that also includes a send-later option (getmailbird.com).

→ Apple Mail: Try a third-party service called MailButler (mailbutler.io).

→ Gmail: Click the down arrow on the send button to reveal "schedule send."

Why Do We Work So Much?

To achieve a better work-life balance, it's useful to examine why we work so much, since in my experience, no one ever intends to work too much.

A lot of my clients tell me that they "have to" work as

much as they do. There are usually two reasons they believe
they have to do this:

 They think long hours are required based on the volume
of work they have.

2 They believe other people expect them to always be
available.

If your team believes that long work hours are required,
they may not have the skills they need to handle their workflow effectively. A workflow management system is a collection of habits and behaviors that help organize all the details
of a person's personal and professional life. My workflow management system is detailed in my Empowered Productivity
book series. Once your team is using a workflow management
system, it becomes much easier to tell whether their volume
of work is appropriate.

Burnout

Recently, the World Health Organization validated something that all busy professionals know about today's work culture: **burnout is very real.**

The WHO added burnout to its handbook of medical

diagnoses. It defines burnout as "a syndrome…resulting from chronic workplace stress that has not been successfully managed." The handbook describes the symptoms of burnout as feelings of depletion or exhaustion, feelings of mental distance from or negativity about one's job, and reduced effectiveness at work.[v]

The symptoms of burnout are virtually the same as the symptoms of disengagement, which Gallup describes as being "unhappy and unproductive at work and liable to spread negativity to coworkers."[vi]

Here's why you need to care now: extrapolating Gallup's statistics results in a cost of 34 percent of an employee's annual salary being lost to burnout.[vii] Multiply that by the number of people in your organization (because burnout rates have only been increasing since the pandemic), and that's how much burnout could be costing your company right now.

Causes of Burnout

Burnout and work-life balance are two sides of the same coin. Working too much is a primary cause of burnout. That's why I've dedicated so much of this book to solving the challenges of working too much.

But working too much is not the only cause. I'll share some others here to help you evaluate whether you need to call in professionals to address them.

High pressure. All companies have periods of high demand, where employees are expected to step up to meet the challenge. But these need to be balanced with periods of lighter workloads. A client who was a leader at a pharmaceutical company told me, "It's been 'crunch time' at the company for the entire seven years I've worked here." This isn't sustainable and is likely damaging your company's performance, bottom line, and reputation with potential hires.

Toxic coworkers/culture. A work environment that is characterized by drama, politics, ridicule, bullying, gossip, humiliation, and blame creates a fast path to burnout and also many other types of dysfunction.

Emotionally taxing job. Jobs in some industries, like health care and social services, are more likely to lead to burnout. Human resources professionals who routinely help employees through difficult situations can also face this type of burnout.

Don't Mistake Burnout for an Attitude Problem

Leadership too often dismisses disengaged, negative employees as having an "attitude problem," transferring the blame. In some cases, this can certainly be true, but I always encourage leaders to take a look at the underlying causes of this attitude, and remind them that a symptom of burnout is feelings of negativity about one's job.

Stress, exhaustion, and feelings of negativity most certainly impact the work of knowledge workers whose mood and brain functioning are the primary components of high-quality work.

Assessing the Risk of Burnout

The following statements are not a scientific assessment for the risk of burnout. However, based on my experience, leaders who identify with the following statements may be at risk of burnout. If some or all of these statements are true for you, they are likely true for your team as well because of the influence you have as a leader. Use them to assess your own burnout, and assess your team members individually to see if they may be at risk.

→ You never take vacation, or you work when you're on vacation.

→ You're never away from work email for more than six or eight hours at a time (while sleeping).

→ You are generally available to anyone regardless of the day or time.

→ You never shut off your phone or put it in "Do Not Disturb" mode.

→ You have no hobbies, or you can't remember the last time you engaged in your hobby.

→ You often feel exhausted for no particular reason.

→ You're always intending to exercise, but you never seem to be able to work it into your schedule.

→ You work when you're sick.

→ You have very few close relationships beyond your immediate family.

→ Your family members or others close to you are often annoyed by your relationship with your device.

To create a high-functioning team or organization that embraces remote work, you'll need to make work-life balance a priority for your team, and that starts by making it a priority for yourself as a leader.

11

The New Realities
of Office Work

As organizations shift to integrate more remote working, the environment inside corporate offices will also shift. Overwhelming evidence demonstrates that the design of an office impacts the health, well-being, and productivity of its occupants, yet the priority for office design now is more commonly how to accommodate more people in less space, and how to make effective use of the space when the number of people who show up on any given day is unpredictable. This makes sense since office space is expensive, but having unproductive employees is also expensive.

In addition to open offices, which have been growing in popularity for more than a decade, "hot desking" is the newest trend. This means that employees don't have a dedicated work space. They either grab whatever is available when they arrive, or they book time in advance. This is easier as work goes more and more digital, and physical work supplies like pens, paper, staplers, paper clips, and files diminish in importance. In this chapter, I'll uncover ways that these trends impact employees and their ability to get important work done.

The Open Office Debate Is Over

The initial justification for open office floor plans was that fewer walls and more open spaces would facilitate opportunities for creative alliances, innovation, and teamwork. There is very little research that proves this true. In my 2017 book *Work Without Walls*, I explored the question of whether open offices help or hurt the productivity of knowledge workers. I also shared the overwhelming research suggesting that any gains in creativity and collaboration are far outweighed by the productivity losses due to noise, distraction, lack of privacy, and managing perceptions. Knowledge work thrives—at least in part—on undistracted reflection and uninterrupted stretches of thoughtful work. Open office floor plans are not typically designed to balance collaboration with thoughtful, undistracted work time.

> **Idea generation is best done alone, whereas group discussions are ideal to evaluate ideas and generate consensus.**

But the question of whether open offices support or undermine productivity is no longer relevant. I don't think businesses are going back to majority private offices in the foreseeable future—business has become accustomed to the cost savings offered by open floor plans. It's true that collaboration is a part of knowledge work, but it's not clear cut. For example, group discussions can actually dampen creativity and originality. Groupthink takes over via a process called "anchoring," which means that early ideas have disproportionate influence over the rest of the conversation. Idea generation is best done alone, whereas group discussions are ideal to evaluate ideas and foster consensus. Idea generation is just one of many aspects of knowledge work that requires quiet, thinking space.

So while open office floor plans are likely here to stay, it's time to bring some balance to the design and recognize that quiet, undistracted thinking is a big part of knowledge work. Our work spaces should reflect this.

Here are some low-cost, low-effort adjustments you can make to an existing open office floor plan—or if you happen to be designing your new office now—to make it a more productive space for your employees.

Control

Employees in an open office can feel helpless because they lack control over their environment. That helplessness can hurt satisfaction, engagement, and productivity. The open office takes away control over attention, space, and privacy.

Control over Attention—Do Not Disturb

In an open office, team members can feel like they need to be available to anyone at any time. There are two major problems with this. The first is that it typically results in constant interruptions from coworkers, preventing brainpower momentum and thoughtful work. The second problem is that a key to managing one's attention is the ability to control one's environment. This can feel impossible in an open office.

To make an open floor plan conducive for deep work, each employee should be empowered to control their environment using a "Do Not Disturb" signal. This could be a sign, a flag, or even headphones.

For this practice to work, you and your team members not only have to identify the "Do Not Disturb" signal, but also need to demonstrate your commitment to it. If you leave your sign up or your headphones on all day, every day, they will lose their effectiveness. If you work with others, you'll need to be available at least some of the time. Also, if you convey the message that you prefer not to be disturbed, then people interrupt you anyway and you give them what they need, that's teaching them that you aren't serious about the message. You have to honor the boundaries you create and use them judiciously. When you do, your coworkers will fall in line.

Here are additional guidelines for rolling out a "Do Not Disturb" practice at your organization.

When a sign/flag is up. Do not approach the team member's desk. This includes for issues such as quick questions, signatures, discussion of nonurgent matters, and unscheduled vendors/visitors. The team member is signaling to the office that they are working on brainpower momentum and should not be interrupted. Here are some alternatives to interrupting them:

→ Simply wait until a later time when their signal is removed.

→ Make a note on your task list of what you wanted to speak

with them about. For example, "Joe: ask him how the client meeting went."

→ Email them with your issue or request and/or schedule a time on their calendar to meet for discussion.

→ Create an audio recording of the issue you want to discuss with them, and send it via email with a request to respond by a specific date.

When a "Do Not Disturb" signal is in use, the team member should also be controlling their technology, with all notifications silenced on all devices. Remember that email is for asynchronous communication, so do not expect an immediate answer. Help your colleague with specific but brief subject lines, such as "response requested by Wednesday."

Only interrupt team members in the case of an emergency (an urgent matter that requires immediate attention). As discussed in chapter 6, what constitutes an "urgent matter" should be clearly defined for the team, because in most businesses, there are very few truly urgent matters.

The length of time a signal is in use should vary by employee. Some team members need more undistracted work time than others due to the nature of their jobs. Optimal increments typically range from about fifteen minutes to about ninety minutes but can be shorter or longer in some cases.

Don't use a "Do Not Disturb" signal to signify breaks, including lunch. Encourage team members to leave their desks during these times.

Communicate with internal and external contacts regarding this new practice of "Do Not Disturb" times. It may be necessary for you to reset expectations. If contacts are used to immediate responses, for example, consider adding a line to the signature block in your email that reads something like, "I only check messages periodically throughout the day. If your message is of a more urgent or time-sensitive nature, please XXX." (How do you want clients and contacts to behave if they have an emergency? This should be a different medium than "normal" communication, so, for example, you might suggest they ask the receptionist to track you down, or route your call to a team member in the department related to their issue.) Communicate to vendors the importance of scheduling appointments and avoiding unannounced/unplanned visits. If you agree to see them when they show up without an appointment, they will continue to engage in this behavior.

Certain departments may need to ensure coverage during "business hours" for urgent and time-sensitive issues. These teams should avoid allowing everyone to be in "Do Not Disturb" mode at the same time.

Be mindful of each other's attention by working to

communicate needs prior to them becoming "urgent," so team members can successfully manage their attention.

Control over Attention—Noise

Since the pandemic, even employers who want everyone back in the office still offer the opportunity to work remotely occasionally. This can provide the opportunity for quiet, undistracted work. But don't make the mistake of assuming that this is true for everyone. Some people have very chaotic home environments and will want or need to work in the office.

However, thoughtful knowledge work is difficult to execute amid a constant cacophony of equipment, conversation, computer keys tapping, phones ringing, and a bustle of constant activity.

If you have the space, create private areas where employees can escape the din and have quiet time to recharge on breaks (even close their eyes for those catnaps discussed earlier) and also to do thoughtful work in an undistracted way. If you have only a little extra room, consider designating the open area as a quiet space, and when employees want to have a discussion, take phone calls, or do other "noisy" work, they need to leave the quiet area.

If space is at a premium, consider investing in noise-canceling headphones for every employee. You can also install a speaker system where you can play nature sounds, as exposure to nature has been shown to reduce stress and provide other benefits. The overhead sounds will provide a natural buffer to the rest of the office noise. Or gift your employees a subscription to a service that allows them to play soothing sounds or music (without words, as our favorite playlists are actually quite distracting).

In considering how much space you have, don't overlook outside spaces. Is there anywhere outside your office space where you can create a comfortable environment? If it's not feasible to design a full-blown outdoor "room," is there at least a place where you could add some picnic tables?

Control over Space

Workers crave their own space, or at least access to a place where they can feel in control of both their personal and professional information. In addition, in a survey of 1,601 workers across North America done by *Harvard Business Review* in 2019, 58 percent of respondents said that better indoor air quality would improve their performance—the top vote getter, and this has become only more important since the coronavirus pandemic.[ii] The second-largest group of respondents (50 percent) voted for exposure to natural light. Additional responses included a view of the outdoors and control over temperature.

In an open space, it's impossible to provide the combination of these things that would appeal to everyone, but a few ideas might help:

→ Consider personal desk lamps instead of, or at least in addition to, overhead lighting.

→ Expand your space into the outdoors around your office.

→ If expanding outdoors isn't an option, look for ways to bring the outdoors in. If your space doesn't have access to natural light, consider full-spectrum light bulbs. Potted plants can provide some exposure to nature in addition to dampening sound. Consider nature as the theme of your office decor.

Control over Work Areas

A new office structure has emerged in the last decade with the rise of coworking spaces, known as hot desking. This is where employees are not assigned a specific desk but can sit anywhere that's available while they are in the office whether for an hour or a full day.

The downside of hot desking is that if workers lack their own space entirely, they're constantly distracted by having to think about their workspace every day, according to Dr. Art Markman, a social psychology professor at the University of

Texas at Austin. Because it's harder for these workers to put anything on autopilot, Markman says, they're less efficient. For example, instead of just mindlessly reaching for a pen, a worker has to disrupt his task to look for the pen cup.

This is becoming less of a problem as the supplies workers need to do their jobs are practically down to just a laptop. But what about coats, snacks, notebooks, and accessories like external monitors, keyboards, mice, video cameras, and printers? Will employees need to take everything with them when they leave for lunch?

Hot desking can be a way to make the most efficient use of office space when the number of employees using a space, and for how long, is unpredictable. But in this situation, consider outfitting each workstation with a monitor, an Ethernet connection for internet, a desk lamp, keyboard, and mouse, and a drawer that can be locked (although you may have to be clear that locks must be removed at the end of every workday).

Control over Privacy

If your work spaces—temporary or permanent—aren't all in open areas but some walls exist, be cautious with glass walls. These create a "fishbowl effect," making employees feel like they are always under scrutiny. As a result, they may spend time managing impressions: worrying about what it looks like they're doing instead of just focusing on their work. The upside of glass walls is that they make the space bright, so consider frosted or distorted film, strategically placed to offer privacy but still let in light.

Knowledge work has left the confines of the corporate office—at least for some employees, some of the time—for the foreseeable future. Remote work is here to stay, and that means that corporate office space will require more adjustments to balance necessity with value. For example, most small businesses won't be able to afford to keep a space that is large enough for every person all the time. Yet the amount of space needed and the time the space will be used will be unpredictable.

I believe that the location of work and office environments will continue to be in flux well into this decade. I've written this chapter as a reference guide that leaders can refer to often as the situation continues to evolve.

12

Measuring the Productivity of Knowledge Work

It's time that we leave behind outdated notions about what constitutes productivity—such as constant availability, face time at the office, excessive work hours, and a relentless pace—that we now know are detrimental and unsustainable.

Forward-thinking businesses can position themselves to thrive by embracing the truth that the productivity of knowledge workers depends on factors that aren't typically considered, such as their well-being and state of mind, their work environment, and their opportunities for downtime and disconnection. By implementing suggestions from this book, it's possible for leaders like you to gain increased insight into the current state of your organization's productivity and take steps that will lead to improvement.

Defining Productivity

In the absence of research-based and other proven, adaptable quantitative knowledge worker productivity metrics, I advise my clients to rely on qualitative metrics. In my experience, they are common sense and reliable, and they result in improved performance.

The word *productive* is defined as "achieving or producing a significant amount or result." Since *productive* has broad application, we can narrow this definition for knowledge work to "achieving a significant result."

How much progress you make on the results that are significant to you in a given time frame equals how productive you are, and the significance changes with the time horizon.

If I were to ask you at the end of today, "What were your significant results?" you'd likely give me a different answer than if I asked you the same question at the end of the week. Or at the end of the year, the end of the decade, or the end of your lifetime.

If I asked you what was significant to you at the end of your life, I expect you would say things like this:

→ I had an impact.

→ I made a difference.

→ I was kind.

→ I loved.

→ I was loved.

So to me, productivity means everything from achieving the most significant thing on your to-do list today to the kind of person you are and the kind of life you lead and everything you would consider significant in between. It's why I'm so passionate about it and why I love working with leaders—because this multiplies my reach. If I can help leaders wield their significant influence wisely, then I can help impact exponentially more people's lives.

Have you ever had the experience of going to work knowing that there were just two or three really important things you had to get done that day? They are weighing on you as you start your day, but before you know it, it's four o'clock, and you're dismayed (and a little astonished) to discover that you haven't had a chance to tackle those things yet! This means you've relinquished control of your day to other people's needs and demands, which is detrimental to your own daily productivity.

Now consider a larger scenario. Have you ever reflected at

the end of a year, or around New Year's Day, or on a birthday, and found yourself thinking, "Wow, another year has gone by, and I still haven't made any real progress on XXX." You haven't gotten the promotion, you didn't go back to school, you didn't start the side business, or you've made no progress on your bucket list. If you've ever found yourself a little disappointed that you haven't made any progress on those life goals that you've set for yourself, then you have experienced how this lack of control over your daily productivity is impacting your ability to achieve your larger goals.

The same experience happens with departmental and organization-wide goals. Employees get so involved in daily "busyness" that important but seemingly less urgent priorities languish.

When you define productivity as progress on results that you and your employees deem significant, you separate busyness from productivity, clarify for your team members what you expect of them, empower everyone to resist the temptation of constant communication, and offer useful metrics for evaluating team member and departmental progress.

Examine Unconscious Calculations

Individual habits shape corporate culture, yet the current habits of employees—even successful employees—are not sufficient for the new realities of the business world, and the skills gap is leaving knowledge workers exhausted. These habits are based on the unconscious calculations I've referenced throughout this book—superficial beliefs that guide our behavior, often without our realization. They are explanations my clients give me for their behavior, but once they say them out loud, they realize they have never examined these beliefs. They also realize that many may not be true, and that they are guiding behaviors in ways that are not supportive to their own productivity and success.

Here are some additional examples of unconscious calculations and the unproductive habits they often create. See how many may be guiding your own habits, or your team's habits, and whether examination would change some of your behaviors.

→ It's too distracting (or I have too many meetings) to get any important work done during the day, so the only opportunity for me to make progress on this important work is when no one is bothering me. (The resulting habit is that you work frequently either late in the evenings, in the very early morning, on the weekends, or all three!)

→ Most communication requires an immediate response, and responding immediately means that I am providing good service to internal and external customers. (The resulting habit is leaving all communication channels open, checking every new message as it arrives. This prevents sustained attention on anything, and caused you to end the workday feeling frazzled.)

→ An open-door policy means everyone is available to anyone at any time for any reason. (The resulting habit is leaving my door open and/or allowing interruptions all day. Recall from chapter 4 how this is both detrimental to team member productivity and undermines employee confidence when leader behaviors are based on this unconscious calculation.)

→ My employees will figure out how to get their work done. (Without proper training, their behaviors come about out of necessity, without intention, and the results are bad habits that lead to stress and burnout.)

→ More communication (and communication tools) is better. (Recall from chapter 6 that without specific guidelines about which tool to use in which situation, the volume of communication will increase dramatically, but it's effectiveness will decrease. (The resulting habit is sending a message in multiple different formats, such as a text that reads "I just sent you an email.")

→ As a leader, I need to be available 24/7. (The resulting

habit is "always on" behavior that encourages my team to do the same, which promotes burnout. Recall from the section in chapter 5 on being available less often how this is likely disempowering your team.)

→ As a leader, it's my prerogative to interrupt team members when they want something. (The resulting habit is failing to respect my team's Do Not Disturb signals, promoting an environment of constant distraction. Recall how this interferes with your team's ability to control their environment from the section in chapter 11 on control.)

→ Everyone wants to work from home/Everyone needs to come back to the office. (The resulting habit is making assumptions about what will motivate my team members and make them happy. This is how the media typically reports on postpandemic work realities, but your employees' needs and job roles are as unique as your employees themselves. Work to create fair criteria for remote work policies, and resist a one-size-fits-all solution.)

If any of the above unconscious calculations are influencing how you lead and interact with your employees, hopefully this book has raised your awareness. Now you can make more intentional decisions about your behaviors and how they influence the members of your team.

Knowledge Worker Productivity Metrics

I think of knowledge work in four primary categories. The most common three are appointments on our calendars, tasks that we believe we must complete (often these represent our most important priorities), and communication in all its forms—emails, chats, impromptu phone calls, voicemails, and conversations. These three typically crowd out the fourth category, which may be the most important yet is often not done in an intentional way. It's thinking time—for planning, developing strategies, generating ideas, and giving thoughtful consideration to the state of our projects, our work, and our lives.

Other tasks that come up outside of these four categories of knowledge work are ad hoc requests, and we tend to respond to these requests first. We operate this way for many reasons. First, doing what is asked of us "right now" is easier (especially if the task is clear) than placing it onto a list, thinking it through, and assigning the appropriate priority to it. Second, most people don't have a useful way to store, organize, and prioritize all the tasks they are responsible for completing, so when a request comes in, doing it now feels safer than risking forgetting to do it later. Lastly, these ad hoc requests feel urgent, even though their importance is not typically assessed. This is one of the many reasons it's important for the leader to step in and offer structure on how work gets done, as discussed in chapter 2. This is also why it's critical for team members to learn skills to keep track of tasks. It's an important component of the workflow management system I teach my clients, because in my experience, most people use some combination of apps, notebooks, sticky notes, and flagged emails in an attempt to keep track of their responsibilities. As a result, it's impossible to prioritize and track appropriately.

When teams embrace the combination of workflow and distribution assigned by leaders, and individual responsibility tracking done by employees, the record of daily accomplishment is clear. When you and your team can see on a daily basis how many important tasks you were able to accomplish, your team's productivity will become apparent to all stakeholders. Your team projects will move forward as expected, and your employees will feel a sense of accomplishment at the end of the day, which makes them happier and more engaged.

Ownership of Team Productivity

Each individual should be responsible for tracking progress on their own significant results. As a leader, you should be responsible for tracking progress on departmental results and holding team members accountable. Both of these are easier with personal workflow management skills. However, in my experience, while most knowledge workers are successful, they lack these skills and thus are operating sub-optimally.

Ideally, one leader in the organization would be responsible for ensuring all team members, including leaders, have the skills to track work appropriately. This leader should also lead the charge to ensure that each department is clearly and effectively managing the flow of work through their department and the organization as a whole.

Further, the leader in this role will also evaluate professional development needs and source training, so a Learning and Development professional, on staff or outsourced, can be an option. However, this goes beyond regular professional development, so an HR director who is also responsible for hiring, compensation and benefits, and other personnel needs is likely not the best fit. In many cases, the job belongs to the CEO or, where relevant, the head of remote, as discussed in chapter 2.

Productivity affects individual and organizational success, the ability to attract and retain talent, and the very culture of the organization, and the culture starts at the top. Therefore, the person to ensure that unhealthy, distracted, "always on" behaviors do not thwart a culture of success *must* have a seat at on the executive committee.

Conclusion

Create Your Culture with Intention

Implementing the ideas in this book will empower leaders like you to break free from unproductive habits caused by unconscious calculations. These strategies will help you craft a culture that empowers your team members to fully unleash their genius in service of their own success and your organization's success. Doing so will help all of you feel satisfied at the end of your days, knowing that you've accomplished meaningful work.

> How do your beliefs, values,
> and goals specifically address
> your team's opportunity
> to do their best work?

First, though, you and other leaders will need to assess and improve your own beliefs and habits and how those are shaping the organizational culture, because the message to employees is strongest when you model behaviors that support a culture of productivity. Regardless of the area you're focused on improving, identifying any misalignments between your company culture and your stated beliefs should be your first step.

Do your current mission and vision take knowledge worker productivity into account? How do your beliefs, values, and goals specifically address your team's opportunity to do their best work? In this conversation, it's important to unearth conflicting impressions that have been holding back your efforts to support your team's productivity.

For example, you may identify that your organizational values include creativity and innovation, but leaders and team members have habits and practices that keep everyone teth-ered to email, prevent them from recharging their wells of fresh thinking, and cause them to work in noisy, distracted environments. This environment directly conflicts with your stated values.

Also consider whether you or other leaders in your company are evaluating employees according to whether they're "always on" without considering the quality of their deliverables. Or you may have managers who are overlooking the contributions of those who work at home just because they're not getting "face time."

Using the metric of "progress on significant results" will motivate all leaders to identify the significant results of their individual team members and their department overall. This is usually done through conversations with both superiors and direct reports.

Being intentional about knowledge worker productivity creates an environment where you and your team feel happy, engaged, and motivated rather than scattered, distracted, and overwhelmed. It provides the space for your team members to best apply their unique knowledge, experience, and talents, which you hired them for in the first place. When you're intentional about your culture, you improve the well-being and productivity of your staff—and the company as a whole.

My recommendation is that you use this book as a guide. Tackle one chapter at a time. You might decide to select the issue that is most pressing in the organization and would have the biggest impact by addressing. Or you might decide to select the issue that is the easiest to address, and use the momentum to provide the motivation to continue.

Let's Continue
the Conversation

Thank you for reading! I'm so excited that this content I've been sharing live with leaders for so many years is now accessible in book form and can reach exponentially more people.

If you found this book useful, I would love to continue the conversation with you! I invite you to reach out for a complimentary follow-up call at maurathomas.com/inquire. And if you know a leader at another organization who can benefit from this book, I would be happy to send you a complimentary copy that you can share with them. As books are now judged primarily through online reviews, I would be so grateful if you would put a favorable review on Amazon if you feel it's warranted.

You can read more of my work on my website, maurathomas .com, and you can subscribe at maurathomas.com/subscribe to receive my latest resources directly in your inbox. If you're on LinkedIn, you can find me at http://linkedin.com/in/ mauranevelthomas-productivity-trainer/. If you reach out to connect with me on LinkedIn, please tell me that you read *Everyone Wants to Work Here* so I know that you're a human and not a bot! I look forward to connecting with you soon!

Acknowledgments

Thank you to the wonderful team at Sourcebooks, including my dedicated editor Meg Gibbons, who demonstrates heroic patience and tact in the face of all my new ideas and changes; Liz Kelsch and her marketing team; and also Sabrina Baskey, without whom this book would be full of extraneous quotation marks and commas, spelling errors, and improperly cited quotes!

I also appreciate Rhea Lyons, Carrie Hannigan, and the team at HG Literary. Lastly, I'd like to thank my own team at Regain Your Time, and especially my mom, Rita, my husband, Shawn, and Content Marketing Director extraordinaire, Shana Burg, all of whom were the first eyes after mine on much of this content, and were generous with their feedback.

Notes

Introduction: The Shift to Knowledge Work

i   Adam Ozimek, "Freelance Forward Economist Report," Upwork, December 2, 2021, https://www.upwork.com/research/freelance-forward-2021.

ii   Daniel Goleman, "Caring Leaders, Better Results," Korn Ferry, accessed May 9, 2022, https://www.kornferry.com/insights/this-week-in-leadership/emotional-intelligence-caring-leader.

iii   Kate Morgan, "Why In-Person Workers May Be More Likely to Get Promoted," *BBC*, March 7, 2021, https://www.bbc.com/worklife/article/20210305-why-in-person-workers-may-be-more-likely-to-get-promoted.

iv   "Vacation Time Recharges U.S. Workers, but Positive Effects Vanish Within Days, New Survey Finds," American Psychological Association, June 27, 2018, https://www.apa.org/news/press/releases/2018/06/vacation-recharges-workers.

v   Amy Elisa Jackson, "We Just Can't Unplug: 2 in 3 Employees Report Working While on Vacation," *Insights* (blog), Glassdoor, May 24, 2017, https://www.glassdoor.com/blog/vacation-realities-2017/.

vi   Tera Allas and Bill Schaninger, "The Boss Factor: Making the World a Better Place through Workplace Relationships," *McKinsey Quarterly*, September 22, 2020, https://www.mckinsey.com/business-functions/people-and-organizational-performance/our-insights/the-boss-factor-making-the-world-a-better-place-through-workplace-relationships.

1: The Most Important Job of a Leader Is to Think

i   Shawn Achor, Andrew Reece, Gabriella Rosen Kellerman, and Alexi Robichaux, "9 Out of 10 People Are Willing to Earn Less Money to Do More-Meaningful Work," *Harvard Business Review*, November 6, 2018, https://hbr.org/2018/11/9-out-of-10-people-are-willing-to-earn-less-money-to-do-more-meaningful-work.

ii   Arash Emamzadeh, "The Benefits of Feeling in Control as We Age," *Psychology Today*, July 16, 2018, https://www.psychologytoday.com/us/blog/finding-new-home/201807/the-benefits-feeling-in-control-we-age.

iii   Teresa M. Amabile and Steven J. Kramer, "The Power of Small Wins," *Harvard Business Review*, May 2011, https://hbr.org/2011/05/the-power-of-small-wins.

iv   Cal Newport, "Why Are So Many Knowledge Workers Quitting?" *Office Space* (blog), *New Yorker*, August 16, 2021, https://www.newyorker.com/culture/office-space/why-are-so-many-knowledge-workers-quitting.

v   Paul Hammerness and Margaret Moore, "Train Your Brain to Focus," *Harvard Business Review*, January 18, 2012, https://hbr.org/2012/01/train-your-brain-to-focus.

vi   "Knowledge Worker Productivity: Challenges, Issues, Solutions," GSA Enterprise Transformations, June 2011, https://www.gsa.gov/cdnstatic/KnowledgeWorker Productivity.pdf.

vii Gloria Mark, Daniela Gudith, and Ulrich Klocke, "The Cost of Interrupted Work: More Speed and Stress," Proceedings of the 2008 Conference on Human Factors in Computing Systems, Florence, Italy, April 5–10, 2008, https://www .ics.uci.edu/~gmark/chi08-mark.pdf.

3: Changing a Culture of Urgency

i   "Is Multitasking More Efficient? Shifting Mental Gears Costs Time, Especially When Shifting to Less Familiar Tasks," American Psychological Association, August 5, 2001, http://www.umich.edu/~bcalab/articles/APAPressRelease2001.pdf.

ii   Cal Newport, "A Modest Proposal: Eliminate Email," *Harvard Business Review*, February 18, 2016, https://hbr.org/2016/02/a-modest-proposal-eliminate-email.

5: A Leadership Formula to Empower Teams

i   Erik Gonzalez-Mulé and Bethany Cockburn, "Worked to Death: The Relationships of Job Demands and Job Control with Mortality," *Personnel Psychology* 70, no. 1 (Spring 2017): 73–112, https://doi.org/10.1111/peps.12206.

ii   David Hassell, "10 Must-Ask Questions to Supercharge Your Leadership," *15five* (blog), accessed May 9, 2022, https://www.15five.com/blog/10-leadership -questions/.

6: Take Vacation Seriously

i   Kathryn Isham, "Importance of Taking a Vacation," *Thrive* (blog), Allina Health, June 15, 2021, https://www.allinahealth.org/healthysetgo/thrive/importance -of-taking-a-vacation.

ii   Sian Beilock, "Why You Need to Take a Vacation: Three Science-Backed Reasons," *Forbes*, August 2, 2021, https://www.forbes.com/sites/sianbeilock/2021/08/02 /why-you-need-to-take-a-vacation-three-science-backed-reasons/.

iii Tom Popomaronis, "Science Says You Shouldn't Work More Than This Number of Hours a Week," *Inc.*, May 9, 2016, https://www.inc.com/tom-popomaronis /science-says-you-shouldnt-work-more-than-this-number-of-hours-a-day.html.

iv   Shawn Achor, "Are the People Who Take Vacations the Ones Who Get Promoted?" *Harvard Business Review*, June 12, 2015, https://hbr.org/2015/06 /are-the-people-who-take-vacations-the- ones-who-get-promoted.

v   "The State of American Vacation 2018," U.S. Travel Association, https://www

.ustravel.org/system/files/media_root/document/StateofAmericanVacation 2018.pdf.

vi   Tony Schwartz and Christine Porath, "Your Boss's Work-Life Balance Matters as Much as Your Own," *Harvard Business Review*, July 10, 2014, https://hbr.org /2014/07/your-bosss-work-life-balance-matters-as-much-as-your-own.

vii   Robert Glazer, "Why This CEO Pays Employees Up to $750 to Unplug on Vacation," *Fast Company*, April 16, 2019, https://www.fastcompany.com /90335109/why-this-ceo-pays-employees-up-to-750-to-unplug-on-vacation.

viii Gabrielle Olya, "Addicted to Work: 82% of Americans Admit to Working on Vacation," GOBankingRates, July 13, 2021, https://www.gobankingrates.com/money/ jobs/addicted-to-work-82-percent-americans-admit-working-on-vacation/.

ix   Richard Branson, "Why We're Letting Virgin Employees Take as Much Holiday as They Want," *Richard Branson's Blog*, Virgin, September 22, 2014, https://www .virgin.com/branson-family/richard-branson-blog/why-were-letting-virgin -staff-take-much-holiday-as-they-want.

x   Justin Bariso, "Netflix's Unlimited Vacation Policy Took Years to Get Right. It's a Lesson in Emotional Intelligence," *Inc.*, September 14, 2020, https://www.inc .com/justin-bariso/netflixs-unlimited-vacation-policy-took-years-to-get-right -its-a-lesson-in-emotional-intelligence.html.

7: How Remote and Hybrid Work Are Changing Business

i   Alicia Sasser Modestino, Jamie J. Ladge, Addie Swartz, and Alisa Lincoln, "Childcare Is a Business Issue," *Harvard Business Review*, April 29, 2021, https://hbr.org/2021/04/childcare-is-a-business-issue.

ii   Paul J. Zak, "The Power of a Handshake: How Touch Sustains Personal and Business Relationships," *Huffington Post*, October 30, 2008, https://www .huffpost.com/entry/the-power-of-a-handshake_b_129441.

8: Necessary Commitments for Successful Remote and Hybrid Teams

i   Ginger Pinholster, "Sleep Deprivation Described as a Serious Public Health Problem," American Association for the Advancement of Science, March 14, 2014, https://www.aaas.org/news/sleep-deprivation-described-serious-public -health-problem.

ii   Eric Suni and Dr. Nilong Vyas, "How Lack of Sleep Impacts Cognitive Performance and Focus," Sleep Foundation, updated April 29, 2022, https://www .sleepfoundation.org/sleep-deprivation/lack-of-sleep-and-cognitive-impairment.

iii   Anthony J. Porcelli and Mauricio R. Delgado, "Stress and Decision Making: Effects on Valuation, Learning, and Risk-Taking," *Current Opinion in Behavioral Sciences* 14 (2017): 33–39, https://doi.org/10.1016/j.cobeha.2016.11.015.

iv   Teresa M. Amabile and Steven J. Kramer, "The Power of Small Wins," *Harvard Business Review*, May 2011, https://hbr.org/2011/05/the-power-of-small-wins.

10: Work-Life Balance

i   Steven I. Weiss, "He Built a $3 Billion Business to Solve Calendar Headaches. Here's His Vision for the Future of Meetings," *Inc.*, March/April 2022, https://www.inc.com/magazine/202203/steven-i-weiss/tope-awotona-calendly-meetings-productivity.html.

ii   John Pencavel, "The Productivity of Working Hours," Discussion Paper No. 8129, April 2014, https://docs.iza.org/dp8129.pdf.

iii   Andrew Merle, "This Is How Many Hours You Should Really Be Working," Work Life, January 4, 2022, https://www.atlassian.com/blog/productivity/this-is-how-many-hours-you-should-really-be-working.

iv   Roy Maurer, "Remote Employees Are Working Longer Than Before," Society for Human Resource Management (SHRM), December 16, 2020, https://www.shrm.org/hr-today/news/hr-news/pages/remote-employees-are-working-longer-than-before.aspx.

v   "Burn-Out an 'Occupational Phenomenon': International Classification of Diseases," World Health Organization, May 28, 2019, https://www.who.int/news/item/28-05-2019-burn-out-an-occupational-phenomenon-international-classification-of-diseases.

vi   Steve Crabtree, "Worldwide, 13% of Employees Are Engaged at Work," Gallup, October 8, 2013, https://news.gallup.com/poll/165269/worldwide-employees-engaged-work.aspx.

vii   Paul Petrone, "How to Calculate the Cost of Employee Disengagement," LinkedIn blog, March 24, 2017, https://www.linkedin.com/business/learning/blog/learner-engagement/how-to-calculate-the-cost-of-employee-disengagement.

11: The New Realities of Office Work

i   Rebecca Greenfield, "Brainstorming Doesn't Work; Try This Technique Instead," *Fast Company*, July 29, 2014, http://www.fastcompany.com/3033567/agendas/brainstorming-doesnt-work-try-this-technique-instead.

ii   Jeanne C. Meister, "Survey: What Employees Want Most from Their Workspaces," *Harvard Business Review*, August 26, 2019, https://hbr.org/2019/08/survey-what-employees-want-most-from-their-workspaces.

12: Measuring the Productivity of Knowledge Work

i   Brandon Rigoni and Bailey Nelson, "Do Employees Really Know What's Expected of Them?" Gallup, September 27, 2016, https://news.gallup.com/businessjournal/195803/employees-really-know-expected.aspx.

Index

activity, physical. *See* movement/
  exercise/physical activity
after-hours emails, xvi, 147–150
asynchronous communication, 30,
  45, 112, 161. *See also* emails
  avoiding video meeting fatigue
    and, 129
  benefits of, 24, 120, 122–123
  brainstorming and, 128–129
  DO system, 35
  Doist, 35–37
  email as, 161
  good uses for, 124
  guidelines for, 127
  moving to, 111, 135–136
  self-serve information and,
    19–20
  tools for, 123–124 (*See also*
    Twist)
Boss for a Day, 83
brainpower momentum, 6–8, 55,
  159, 160
brainstorming, 128–129
burnout, 71, 76, 79, 137
  assessing risk of, 154–155
  causes of, 11–12, 71, 89, 103,
    108, 144, 152–153, 173–174
  preventing, 4, 34, 95, 123, 140,
    143
  symptoms of, 152, 154
calculations, unconscious, xi–xii,

43, 45, 171–174, 178
chat. *See also* Slack; Twist
  connecting beyond work and,
    39
  disabling during meetings, 134
  as distraction, 12, 28–29
  downsides of, 58
  interference with "real work," 4
  need for guidelines, 30–31
  out-of-office message, 84
  sharing information via, 25–27
  used as synchronous
    communication, 27
  using as asynchronous tool, 123
childcare, 104
communication, asynchronous.
    See asynchronous
    communication
communication, synchronous. *See*
  synchronous communication
communication guidelines, 86,
  127, 146, 147, 149, 173. *See also*
  Do Not Disturb
  lack of, 26
  need for, 30–31
culture of urgency, 28, 47, 50, 54
  changing, 40
  effects of, 41–42
CYA culture, 67
distributed work. *See* remote
  work

DO (Doist objectives) system, 35–37
Do Not Disturb
    after hours, 127, 146, 147
    need for, 155
    signal, 159–163
Doist, 34–37
    DO system, 35–37
    Todoist, 35, 36
    Twist, 35–36
Eikenberry, Kevin, 135
emails, after-hours, xvi, 147–150
Empowered Productivity System/
    Series, 24, 82, 151
exercise. See movement/exercise/
    physical activity
15five, 68, 95
flextime, 73
    as always on, 143–147
fully distributed work. See remote
    work
Glazer, Robert, 87
Hassell, David, 68
Hastings, Reed, 96
hot desks, vii, 104, 156–157,
    165–166
IBM, 83
knowledge work, definition of,
    vii, ix
Mailbird, 150
MailButler, 150
Mark, Gloria, 12
Markman, Art, 166
meetings, 125, 126
    avoiding video meeting fatigue,
        129–136
    platforms for, 131–132

    productive, 130
    reducing time spent in, 129
    settings for, 132–133
mentor in hindsight, 62, 69–70
Mercedes-Benz, 85
metrics
    business success, xii, 100
    customer service, 45–46
    face time and, 92
    individual success/happiness,
        100
    productivity, 108, 169–177
    specifying, 92
micromanaging, 62–63
Microsoft Outlook, 42, 150
Microsoft Teams, 4, 32, 47, 123,
    129
movement/exercise/physical
    activity, 113, 114, 116–117,
    130, 142, 155
multitasking, xii, 10, 11, 41
Netflix, 96
Newport, Cal, 6, 43
open office, 156, 157–159
physical activity. See movement/
    exercise/physical activity
progress principle, 119
remote work, xi
    as all-consuming, viii
    "business hours" and, 23
    commitments for, 111–120
    communication and, 121–136
    defining, 101–102
    distributed, 101
    efficiency in, 29
    factors involved in, 102–110
    fully distributed, 37–39, 101

hybrid, 38, 101–102
metrics for, xii, 99–100
remote-first, 34–36
reputation capital, 51–54
schedule send feature, 146, 150
Slack, 4, 32, 47, 87, 123, 146. *See also* chat
sleep, 113, 114–116, 148, 150
synchronous communication
brainstorming and, 128
chat treated as, 27
email treated as, 27, 47–48, 49–50
emphasis on, 112
guidelines for, 126–127
remote work and, 121–122

shifting away from, 19, 20–21, 29–30
Slack used for, 123
tools for, 124–125
using Twist for, 31
time off, unlimited, 80, 87–97
trust, xiv, 61, 62, 63, 68, 76, 87, 90, 94, 105–108, 147
Twist, 30–34, 35–36, 124
unconscious calculations, xi–xii, 43, 45, 171–174, 178
unlimited vacation time, 80, 87–97
Vanderkam, Laura, 141
Warrington, Chase, 35, 37
Zappos, 59
Zoom, 122, 123, 125, 128, 129

About the Author

This is my sixth book, and there is so much about my professional background out in the world already that I feel like adding it here too is just getting excessive. I feel truly fortunate that my circumstances, luck—and yes, hard work—have offered me opportunities and a level of success that have enabled me to design a beautiful life. I'm grateful for it all every day, and I try hard not to take any of it for granted. I'm a third-generation American, the daughter of a strong, independent single mom who taught elementary school for over thirty years. I'm also the granddaughter of a mischievous, big-band-loving, World War II Army vet who drove a truck after his service to support his family, and a generous, wise daughter of Italian immigrants, the youngest of eleven children, who worked as a waitress for spending money she used to spoil her family. I've had a core group of friends since grade school, and while I'm a proud Bostonian at heart, my husband Shawn and I have called Austin, Texas, home for over twenty years. If there is anything else you'd like to know about my professional history, my wonderful clients, or my other works, you can find it all at maurathomas.com.